W9-CII-790

Louis Agassiz Fuertes
& the singular
beauty of birds

Foreword by Dean Amadon
Introduction by Roger Tory Peterson

Louis Agassiz Fuertes & the singular beauty of birds

Paintings, drawings, letters
assembled and edited by
Frederick George Marcham

Harper & Row, Publishers
New York   Evanston   San Francisco   London

To Mary Fuertes Boynton

LOUIS AGASSIZ FUERTES & THE SINGULAR
BEAUTY OF BIRDS

All rights reserved. No part of this book may be used or reproduced in any manner whatsoever without written permission, except in the case of brief quotations embodied in critical articles and reviews. For information address Harper & Row, Publishers, Inc., 49 East 33rd Street, New York, N.Y. 10016. Published simultaneously in Canada by Fitzhenry & Whiteside, Limited, Toronto.

FIRST EDITION 1971

STANDARD BOOK NUMBER: 06-012775-9

LIBRARY OF CONGRESS CATALOG CARD NUMBER: 76-156537

ALL ARTWORK PHOTOGRAPHED BY ELMER S. PHILLIPS

DESIGNED BY BETTY BINNS

Production coordinated by Chanticleer Press, Inc., New York
Printed and bound by Amilcare Pizzi, S.p.A., Milan, Italy

Contents

For the past ten years I have studied the paintings, drawings, and letters of Louis Agassiz Fuertes with a view to making a selection from them that would show in the highest form his ability "to discover and crystallize truth"—the phrase is his own.

The letters I have used are the property of his daughter, Mrs. Mary Fuertes Boynton. I have chosen them from some hundreds of his letters which belong to her and which she has generously allowed me to study and use. They are not only the source of the text but also of much of the material for the biographical essay. Mrs. Boynton also allowed me to choose from her collection of her father's pictures, consisting of one thousand or so pencil sketches together with a few water colors and wash drawings. These pictures were the larger part of a mass of papers which Fuertes accumulated in his studio over the years. The remainder of this collection became, with a few exceptions, the property of The American Museum of Natural History in New York.

I have used a number of water colors and drawings from the collection of The American Museum of Natural History. The other pictures reproduced in this book come from three collections. The owners of these are the Government of the United States, the Field Museum of Natural History, Chicago, and Cornell University. All five owners have given me permission to reproduce the pictures I have chosen from their collections.

I wish to thank many people whose help and patience over a long period of time made this book possible: Mrs. Mary Fuertes Boynton and her brother, Sumner Fuertes, who gave me permission to use their father's paintings, drawings, and letters and encouraged me as the work went forward.

The officers of the Federal Government: in particular, in the Department of the Interior, Fish and Wildlife Service, the director of the Bureau of Sports Fisheries and Wildlife, Dr. John Gottschalk; Dan Saults, chief of the Office of Conservation Education; and Bob Hines, the staff artist of the bureau, who served as my guide and adviser. Also to Dr. Richard H. Manville, director of the Bird and Mammal Laboratories Division of Wildlife Research, the Smithsonian Institution.

The officers of the Field Museum of Natural History, Chicago; in particular Dr. A. L. Rand, chief curator of zoology, and W. Peter Fawcett, the librarian.

The faculty members associated with the Cornell Laboratory of Ornithology at Cornell University; particularly Dr. O. S. Pettingill, Jr., Dr. J. L. Tate, Jr., and Dr. D. A. Lancaster. Professor Emeritus P. Paul Kellogg of the Laboratory of Ornithology, Cornell University, supplied important information about Fuertes and gave me much encouragement.

Finally, and with the acknowledgment of an extra burden of debt, I thank Dr. Dean Amadon, Lamont Curator of Birds and chairman of the Department of Ornithology, The American Museum of Natural History, New York. Also the director of the museum, Dr. Thomas Nicholson, and Mrs. Allston Flagg, curator of the Fuertes Collection in the museum.

The persons named above supported my requests for opportunities to study their collections; later they helped me gain permission to reproduce the pictures I selected. Cornell University's Olin Library gave assistance of another kind. Dr. C. Herbert Finch, curator and University archivist, Barbara Shepherd, and Robert R. Jones helped me to find my way about in the Fuertes letters and drawings which are in their care and they served as custodians of the Fuertes pictures which I brought together from other collections and put in their safekeeping. My warm thanks go to them.

Professor Emeritus Elmer S. Phillips of Cornell University has photographed the pictures used in this book. His great knowledge of photography, his skill, his enthusiasm, and his companionship have given to the last stages of preparing this book new pleasure. Nahum J. Waxman, editor, Harper & Row, has given firm guidance and wise counsel.

F. G. M.

Foreword by Dean Amadon

Louis Agassiz Fuertes is regarded by many as the foremost illustrator of birds of all time. His strength, without question, was his matchless, intimate bird portraits, based on rigorous fieldwork and on the closest observation of the attitudes and characteristics of each creature. The fieldwork, of course, was followed by even more patient, arduous labors before the easel, with field sketches and specimens beside him, for Fuertes was a brilliant technician as well as an observer.

Fuertes' native abilities with brush and pencil, wedded to his single-minded devotion, attracted the attention of naturalists from the very beginning of his career. He became first the protégé of Elliott Coues, perhaps the most brilliant American ornithologist of all time; after Coues' death, Frank M. Chapman of The American Museum of Natural History became the artist's friend and mentor.

Above and beyond his abilities as an artist, Fuertes was a remarkably creative man. Although he did not publish a great deal, his speech and his letters—the latter often charmingly illustrated with drawings— were as sparkling as his art. And the letters are not only sparkling; they convey something of the warmth, joyfulness, and intensity of spirit—charisma, as we might call it today—that won him a host of friends. How fortunate to have selections from his letters published now in combination with his brilliant paintings!

It is also fortunate that Professor F. G. Marcham, former chairman of the Department of History at Cornell University, has undertaken to bring to a wider audience an appreciation of his gifted colleague Fuertes. Professor Marcham is an authority on art and was a professional in that field before turning to history. In his quest to bring together the finest works of Fuertes, he has traveled far and wide, for the originals are scattered. And, once the paintings were found, the selection of those that would be included in the present volume and the complicated arrangements for their use occupied not days or weeks but literally years of effort. Nor should one forget Professor Marcham's text, which is in many respects the finest appreciation of Fuertes as a man and as an artist yet to appear.

Professor Marcham first shared his plan for this project with me some years ago, and from the beginning I admired the diligence and the insight with which he examined the considerable collection of Fuertes originals at The American Museum of Natural History in New York City. Now, with the keenest satisfaction, I welcome the results of his unstinting labors.

The American Museum of Natural History
New York City
June, 1970

Introduction by
Roger Tory Peterson

Just over forty-five years ago, in November of 1925, I traveled to my first convention of the American Ornithologists' Union. For three days I attended the sessions that were held at The American Museum of Natural History in New York. There I met Ludlow Griscom, who was to become the dean of American birdwatchers; Francis Lee Jaques, who had just started his distinguished art career at the museum; Arthur Allen of Cornell, one of the world's first professors of ornithology; and even such legendary pioneers as Frank Chapman and Edward Howe Forbush. But for a seventeen-year-old from a small town, who had never before met any of the high ornithological "brass," the climax came when I was introduced to Louis Agassiz Fuertes.

In the bird art exhibit, on display in one of the halls on the second floor, were two of my own drawings. They were among my very first efforts—a ruby-throated hummingbird and a kingbird, which, I remember, took me three weeks to paint. Just what the great man said about these drawings I do not remember, but I know he was kind. I do remember that to illustrate a point he led me over to a small water color, not one of his own, but a study by the British bird portraitist, Archibald Thorburn. The simple point he wished to make was that a highlight on a bird's dark back could actually be as light in value as the shadow on its white breast (he was a firm advocate of Abbott Thayer's theory of countershading).

Later, as we walked down the broad steps to the first floor of the museum, he reached into his inner coat pocket and withdrew a handful of red sable brushes. Picking out a flat one about half an inch wide

he handed it to me, saying: "Take this; you will find it good for laying in washes." I thanked him and before we parted he added, "And don't hesitate to send your drawings to me from time to time. Just address them to Louis Fuertes, Ithaca, New York."

Actually, I never did send any of my drawings to him for criticism; I had decided to wait until they were worth his time. And so, by delaying, I forfeited a priceless opportunity, for less than two years later Fuertes met his tragic death at a railroad crossing. As for the paint brush, I never used it. I had discovered some white paint caked in the heel at the base of the bristles; the master himself had actually painted with that brush. Therefore, I put it aside as a treasured keepsake.

I have always envied George Miksch Sutton his close contact with Fuertes, for of all the young men, and some not so young, who went to him for inspiration and advice, Fuertes gave most freely to George. Not that he withheld things from the others; certainly not; he was completely unselfish in sharing his ideas and the tricks of the trade. Courtenay Brandreth, now long forgotten, was one of his favored disciples. But in his letters to George Sutton he was more detailed and articulate in defining the principal tenets of his art.

George Sutton, still painting brilliantly in his seventies, has been the main bridge between Fuertes and many of today's leading bird portraitists—not only men of middle years such as Don Eckelberry, Robert Mengel, and John Henry Dick, who have now matured their own distinctive styles, but also gifted younger men such as Robert Verity Clem and Don

Malick, who had not even been born while Fuertes was living. All studied Fuertes' work, but received their early encouragement and criticism from George Sutton.

We can accurately say that there is a "Fuertes school" of bird painting, even to this day, more than four decades after his death. Some may question, of course, whether this is a good thing. Surely it is not if the disciples are only carbon copies of the master. But happily, in this instance, none of Fuertes' followers have slavishly followed his line beyond their twenties. Sutton has gone through at least three well-defined periods of transition since his youth. Clem is another who developed and grew. As a young man not yet twenty he mastered the Fuertes style so well that I could not always tell one of his drawings from an early Fuertes. Today he paints with a feeling for space, more in the fashion of Andrew Wyeth.

Fifty years ago there were relatively few bird illustrators, but amongst them were several whose work was widely published. Allan Brooks, Edmund Sawyer, and Bruce Horsfall come to mind. During this period Fuertes stood head and shoulders above his contemporaries, as had Audubon a century earlier.

Today, in the 1970's, there is far more talent and activity amongst bird artists than we have known previously, in direct proportion, no doubt, to the increased popular interest in birds. It is now possible for quite a number of competent artists to make a very good living painting birds. Some such as Arthur Singer, Fenwick Lansdowne, and Ray Harm may trace their genesis to Audubon. Guy Coheleach, a product of the commercial art world, is a professional in the real sense, and can paint skillfully in almost any tradition. But nearly all American bird artists, directly or indirectly, have been influenced to some extent by the bird portraiture of Fuertes; all save a very few, like the late Francis Lee Jaques, who insisted he was not a feather painter but a painter of the bird's environment.

Several of the world's bird artists whose paintings demand the highest prices today are not by critical standards the best draftsmen or the most innovative or evocative. The thing they seem to have in common is extreme detail; one can put their work under a hand glass, and for that reason their buyers insist they are supreme. One hears the comment "Can't you just feel those feathers?" These finicky portraits often lack the subtleties of form and pterylography, in which Fuertes excelled.

There are, of course, some such as Don Eckelberry and Al Gilbert, who are fine draftsmen with distinctive styles, who do not fiddle but paint with the sure direct touch that Fuertes would have praised.

As one who paints birds and who has been much influenced by Fuertes' approach, I have been fascinated by his early development and particularly by his artistic dilemma, one which has also confounded me—whether to paint birds impressionistically, as the eye sees them, bathed in light and shadow, or to paint them as detailed feather maps devoid of modifying atmosphere (to use Don Eckelberry's terminology, "objective realism vs. intellectual realism"), or to compromise in some way.

Fuertes was born under a lucky star, there is no doubt. At an early age he was befriended by and fell under the influence of Abbott Thayer, who wrote that controversial treatise *Concealing Coloration in the Animal Kingdom.* This was an exposition of the "laws of disguise through color and pattern"—natural camouflage. Fuertes understood this principle thoroughly and was one of Thayer's greatest advocates. He was obviously trying to indoctrinate me when he showed me that painting by Thorburn, and his letters to George Sutton are full of this same persuasive logic. Yet, he seldom practiced the idea himself, for if an artist were really to succeed at it, the beholder would hardly be able to see the bird for the background. During his mid-thirties Fuertes' correspondence reveals the spot he was in: old Abbott Thayer berating him for letting him down by painting birds that stood out from their surroundings, while at the same time Gilbert Grosvenor of the *National Geographic* and Frank Chapman of *Bird-Lore* were sending back drawing after drawing because the bird did not stand out quite enough. In the end, and with some anguish, no doubt, he was realistic enough to make his decision to emphasize the bird itself rather than its environment. Therefore, he usually ignored the third-dimensional play of light and shade in favor of unmodified local color—a concession that most bird portraitists make to the demands of ornithological illustration.

In later years Fuertes expressed a desire to get away from painting mere portraits of birds, those functional book illustrations for which he was in such demand. I remember clearly that day in 1925 at the museum. He had on exhibit a large oil of a great horned owl on the ground against a background of dead leaves, a bold treatment that reminded me of a canvas by Liljefors, the Swede (Plate 60). "This is the way I really like to paint," he said. "I'm going to do more of it from now on."

He never did. He still had some of the plates for *The Birds of Massachusetts* (Vol. III, 1929) to finish when he died at the age of fifty-three. He had just returned from Abyssinia with a portfolio of field sketches that many consider the finest water colors of his career. Because of the accident he was denied at least twenty productive years and the world was denied the many paintings that were locked in his mind.

Old Lyme, Connecticut
December, 1970

Louis Agassiz Fuertes
& the singular
beauty of birds

Biographical essay
by Frederick George Marcham

When the last of his six children was born, Estevan Antonio Fuertes could not decide whether to name him for Ezra Cornell, who had founded the college where he taught, or for Louis Agassiz, the great Harvard naturalist, who had been a visiting professor at the college. He finally settled on Agassiz. In doing so, he also, much to his later distress, pointed the way to a profession and a way of life for his son. From his earliest childhood, the boy was drawn to the study of wildlife, especially birds. When he was still very young, Louis Agassiz Fuertes pored over the original elephant folio edition of Audubon's *Birds of America,* and he later said that from the beginning he understood what Audubon was attempting to achieve because he himself felt the same desire to comprehend and to embody birds.[1]*

Fuertes became, eventually, not only an artist, but an adventurer. One of a hardy generation of naturalists, archaeologists, ethnologists, and highly informed amateur travelers and explorers, he was eager to trek from one end of the western hemisphere to the other to pursue new birds in distant settings. On foot and by mule, by horse, by steamer, and by rail, Fuertes hunted the deep corners of North and South America. "I was born with the itching foot and the sight of a map or even a timetable is enough to stir me all up inside."[2] Gun in hand, he stalked his specimens with all the instincts and accuracy of a hunter, frequently attracting the prize with his perfect imitations of bird songs. Once he brought down his quarry, he became the ornithologist, quickly making careful notes—often mentally—of the fast-fading coloration of the bird

*Superior numbers refer to notes following this essay, page 17.

and the characteristic attitudes of the specimen. In fact, his early attempts at drawing birds were only the means to learn about them.

It is impossible to separate the artist and naturalist from the man. Throughout his life Fuertes collected friends and acquaintances as widely as he collected birds' skins and museum specimens. Known and respected by many of the prominent natural scientists and museum curators of his day, he was also a local fixture in Ithaca, where he made his home. A leader of the Boy Scouts, a Cornell character, a raconteur, lecturer, and musician, Fuertes was a rich and gifted person whose warmth and enthusiasm inspired many otherwise undeveloped young naturalists.

The scope of Fuertes' work is seen in his published works, which range from *Citizen Bird,* a children's book he illustrated in 1897, while still an undergraduate, to *Handbook of Birds of the Western United States* (1902), to *Birds of New York* (1910). The paintings and drawings in these books are to be studied not only for their painstaking accuracy but mainly for their devoted attention to the "personal look" of the birds. It was Fuertes' ardent desire to show birds exactly as they were, beyond just the outward appearance, shape, and size. His exquisitely sophisticated techniques re-created the actual bird. More than an ornithologist, naturalist, and illustrator, Fuertes was an artist who brought to life the birds of three continents and left a permanent record and inspiration to all who would know birds.

Louis Agassiz Fuertes was born on February 7, 1874, the son of Estevan Antonio Fuertes, a professor of

3

Dowitcher, probably Short-billed
Limnodromus griseus
North America
Pencil drawing
approximately 5¼" x 4½"

civil engineering at Cornell University, and the former Mary Stone Perry, a talented musician.

While still a young child, Fuertes showed a keen interest in nature and was particularly fascinated by birds. How he came by this interest no one knows, for certainly his parents did not have it. His mother said that as a child "he violently resented the action of his playmates who intentionally annoyed him by making false associations of the parts of a set of sliced birds, his favorite possession,"[3] and his sister, in an interview, recalled that at the age of eight or nine he would, before disposing of the carcasses of dead birds, "first cut off their wings and handle them with the utmost loving fingers, arranging the webs of every feather in perfection."[4]

Louis studied Audubon's plates and later said that those "wonderful books" were "my greatest delight as a child and for many years were the only works on American birds of which I had any knowledge. It would be hard to estimate their effect upon me, but I am very sure that they were the most potent influence that was ever exerted on my youthful longings to do justice to the singular beauty of birds."[5]

In his attempt to capture and remember the habits and coloration of the first male red crossbill he had ever seen, he drew it. Thus, at the age of fourteen, he inadvertently started his career, for at first drawings were only a method of study. Throughout his teens he continued to sketch, and birds became so much a part of his life that to paint them was second nature. After one of the first showings of his works in Ithaca a lady who had seen them met young Fuertes on the street. "Louis, how do you do it?" she asked. "How do you paint them so exactly?" "But that's the way they are," he answered.[6]

Fuertes also began to compile a life list of species he saw. On the back of each sketch or drawing he made very careful observations of the individual bird, seen alive in the field, confined on the perch, or held dead in his hand. These records won him, at seventeen, associate membership in the American Ornithologists Union, whose active membership was limited to fifty people in the entire United States.

Fuertes' father had planned for his son a career in architecture or engineering, but he could not help noticing the boy's passionate interest in birds and the paintings and drawings that were accumulating in the Fuertes home. Calling upon his associate, the eminent botanist and horticulturist Liberty Hyde Bailey, Professor Fuertes asked, "What would you do with a boy like this?" "Let him go," replied Bailey.[7] Nevertheless, Fuertes enrolled in the Cornell University College of Architecture in 1893. A future in ornithology, then a field in its infancy, was not promising, and the need to prepare for a serious profession prevailed.

Fuertes' student years were not distinguished for their intellectual attainments. Louis was an active undergraduate, joining heartily in fraternity life, contributing to the college humor magazine, and singing in the glee club. It was through the glee club that he met one of the men who most profoundly shaped his career. A fellow member suggested that he introduce

¶A note on nomenclature: The conventions used in assigning genus and species names to the birds and animals in this book conform to best modern usage. In certain instances, therefore, the scientific name, as it appears in a caption, may not agree with Fuertes' own notations on the accompanying painting or drawing.

Black-bellied Plovers
Squatarola squatarola
Holarctic
Wash drawing
approximately 7" x 5½"

Fuertes, whose drawings he had seen, to his uncle, Elliott Coues. Coues was one of the leading ornithologists of the day, and Fuertes said that at his first meeting with Coues he decided that bird painting would be his profession. Coues, for his part, encouraged the young artist and even intervened with his father. More important, Coues offered the young Fuertes, who was only a sophomore, the opportunity to work professionally as an illustrator. He showed Fuertes' paintings to Audubon's granddaughters, exhibited his work at the 1895 AOU meetings, and asked him to illustrate *Citizen Bird,* a children's book Coues was writing with Mabel O. Wright. By 1897, the year Fuertes was graduated from Cornell, he had already illustrated three books. *Citizen Bird* alone contained 111 illustrations.

Louis' work was so distinctive and excellent that Coues, writing in the *New York Nation* in 1896, said, "his pictures are better than Audubon's were to begin with, and we suspect that the mantle has fallen on Mr. Fuertes." In 1897, Coues wrote in *The Osprey,* "I say deliberately, with a full sense of the weight of my words, that there is no one who can draw and paint birds as well as Mr. Fuertes, and I do not forget Audubon himself when I add that America has not produced an ornithological artist of equal possibilities."

Coues, who kept a wise professional eye on Fuertes' career, strongly advised him to attend the AOU meetings in 1896. Fuertes took a week off from his classes —he was then still in his senior year at college—to attend, showing and discussing some of his pictures.

Another participant in those meetings was Abbott

H. Thayer, a prominent artist. Thayer was not present when Fuertes first presented his own paintings, but later in the meetings, when Thayer was lecturing on the protective coloration of birds and mammals, Fuertes carried the discussion further by talking about the purpose of coloration in birds, particularly the vivid colors of many males. His views made such an impression on Thayer that shortly afterward he wrote to Fuertes inviting him to visit and discuss coloration with him. In time, Thayer learned to his great surprise "that you are an artist,"[8] and, later, seeing some of Fuertes' paintings declared, "Yours are the true thing." From Thayer this was high praise, for he added, "Half my life's passion is birds and pictures of them."[9]

So began another friendship which greatly influenced Fuertes. Fuertes gladly took up Thayer's offer of instruction, accepting a subordinate place, and, more than that, entering wholeheartedly into the life of the Thayer family, with whom he spent much time during the next few years at their homes at Monadnock, near Dublin, New Hampshire, and at Scarborough, New York.

Thayer, a man of intense spirit, held before Fuertes, who had had no formal training until this point, the ideal of the great painter, while assuring him that study and practice were necessary. Thayer never doubted his pupil's talent. He wished to train him, for he had received his early instruction in France and, with some justice, believed himself an authority on the art of painting. "You will be amazed," he wrote to Fuertes, "at the end of even a few months of pure, abstract exercise of your sight power, to see how much

Horned Grebe
Podiceps auritus
Holarctic
Wash drawing
approximately 3½″ x 2⅜″

Two pictures of Common Snipe
Capella gallinago
North America
approximately 2½″ x 2½″
and 2½″ x 3½″

nearer you can come to the delicate charm of a bird."[10]

Thayer's urge to dominate and mold was powerful, and yet he was a true educator in that he knew he must draw out the qualities of his pupil, not impose a pattern on him. "I trust," he wrote Louis, "you won't fear my influence as hostile to your individuality."[11] Thayer played his part with such skill that after his death Louis wrote, "I wonder if Uncle Abbott ever knew how much he had been to me, how much more I learned from him than he ever taught me consciously, how much more important than his lessons in painting were his lessons in living." Of his association with the Thayer family he said, "They were my happiest and most uplifting days. Where would I be —and what—if I had not had them?"[12]

Thayer and Coues gave Fuertes the kind of encouragement he could not find at home, for his father still had little faith in his son's chosen field. From these two older men Fuertes received, on the one hand, artistic stimulation and guidance and, on the other, business advice. Thayer taught Fuertes to see as a painter should see; Coues made his work known to publishers, ornithologists, and nature writers. From this time on Fuertes never lacked work, either as a book illustrator or an official painter with biological expeditions.

It was through the naturalists that Fuertes met at the AOU that he became an illustrator for biological expeditions. His first trip was to Florida with the Thayers in the spring of 1898. The next year, at the suggestion of Dr. C. Hart Merriam, chief of the Biological Survey, he was invited on an expedition to Alaska that was an adjunct of an excursion planned by Edward Harriman. In 1901 he was off to Texas with the U.S. Biological Survey under Vernon Bailey, the chief field naturalist of the survey, and in 1902 he made his first trip with Frank M. Chapman of The American Museum of Natural History to the Bahamas, followed by a trip to the West after the 1903 AOU meeting in San Francisco. Chapman was at the time pioneering in the development of habitat displays for the American Museum and made several collecting trips, often with an artist. Over the many years of friendship and active collaboration, Fuertes and Chapman logged sixty thousand miles together.

During this time Fuertes was also actively illustrating a variety of publications, including yearbooks for the Department of Agriculture, articles for the magazine *Outing,* several bird books—among them *Birds of the Rockies* (1902) by Leander S. Keyser; *Handbook of Birds of the Western United States* (1902) by Florence Merriam Bailey, Vernon Bailey's wife; and *The Water Fowl Family* (1903) by Leonard Sanford, Louis B. Bishop, and Theodore S. Van Dyke—and, most important, Elliott Coues' standard work, *Key to North American Birds* (1903), for which he was paid $20 a drawing.

In June 1904, Fuertes married Margaret Sumner of Ithaca, whom he had known for several years, and the young couple began building a house in Ithaca— but not before they went on a bird-collecting honeymoon to Jamaica. This was Margaret Fuertes' first and last trip with her husband, and it is notable for a story she told to her daughter:

As soon as they touched land, she said, Louis was off after birds like a shot, and she hardly saw him again. He found the botanist William

Screech Owl
Otus asio
North America
Wash drawing
approximately 7" x 5¼"

A. Maxon collecting plants for the National Museum . . . and they at once joined forces. . . . The men spent their mornings collecting and their afternoons skinning the day's bag of birds—in the hotel bedroom, the bride choosing to be absent. She thought they might emerge for tea, but they were far too busy; let the tea be sent in to them. On one occasion the bride entered to fetch the tea tray. Louis, both hands be-gooed with the insides of the little tody he was preparing, bent over to pick up with his teeth the last bit of cookie. Madge: "Louis! What are you doing?" Mr. Maxon, enormously amused: "Do you always eat that?" Louis, nonchalant: "Why, it's the best part of the whole bird!"[13]

As Fuertes' daughter goes on to explain, Margaret Fuertes did not believe that accompanying a serious scientist on a rough field trip was a good idea for any woman, for the deprivations which a man, intent on his work, could endure were a true hardship for a woman, who might therefore become a hindrance and a nuisance. She understood her husband's need for travel and never stood in his way. Besides this, she had two children to care for—Sumner, born in 1905, and Mary, born in 1908.

After his marriage, the thought of a long journey often left Fuertes with "remorseful blues."[14] He balanced the pull of home and the excitement of travel, recognizing that "it takes some time to desert one's family and duty and feloniously leave home behind for purely hoggish glutting of bird joys before."[15]

Over the next few years, Fuertes did make a number of field trips, several with Chapman—to Saskatchewan and Alberta in 1907; to Cape Sable and the Cuthbert Rookery in Florida in 1908, there to see the vanishing roseate spoonbills; to Mexico in 1910; to Colombia in 1911; and to Colombia again in 1913. He also went to the Magdalen Islands in 1909 with Dr. Leonard C. Sanford, who was passionately interested in ornithology and who became a friend and champion of Fuertes.

Fuertes' artistic output during the early years of his marriage was steady and, of course, included many illustrations for Chapman. He also began lecturing, and after 1910 this was usually the chief cause of his short absences from Ithaca.

For the rest of his life, however, especially after 1913, Ithaca was Fuertes' base of operations. There he maintained his studio, and there he wholeheartedly entered into the demanding social and community life that made him a leading personality on the Cornell campus and in the town of Ithaca itself. He was a prominent figure in the Boy Scouts and in musical organizations, in which he sang and played. He led the local children on bird walks and in other nature studies. Cornell alumni, when they came back to Ithaca, sought him out as the person they most associated with the university, although he was formally a faculty member for only four years. He was perhaps the most famous alumnus of his generation. There were excitement and an exotic flavor in the Fuertes home, partly from the mementos Fuertes collected—the hundred-pound sack of South American coffee in the closet, the Indian blankets, the bird skins; partly from the continual stream of professors and farmers, children and student artists, who visited the studio; and partly from Fuertes' uncanny ability to fix almost any piece of equipment and imitate almost any bird or animal. Much of his day he spent in his studio with the door open, while neighbors, faculty friends, and visiting ornithologists talked with him as he painted.

Gorilla
Pongo pongo
Africa
Pencil drawing
approximately 9″ x 7″

Their presence did not distract Fuertes, who busied himself with his daily program of illustrations for *Bird-Lore* or a new book or worked on his commissioned paintings in water colors or oils. He was, however, almost always well behind his schedule even though he worked at a prodigious pace. More than a thousand of Fuertes' letters survive, and this is only a fragment of his total correspondence, but they are more than enough to indicate the breadth of his friendships and the warmth and generosity of his personality. He appears to have been one of those people who are constantly delighted by life—an "Oh! and Ah!" father, he once called himself[16]—and this vitality marked all his personal and professional relationships, according to all those who met him, knew him, and gathered with him in his home and studio.

The continuing flow of work was generally enough to keep Fuertes busy and reasonably secure economically. His assignments ranged from government commissions to private commissions for individual paintings. To the large two-volume *Birds of New York* (1910) by Elon Howard Eaton and *Birds of Massachusetts and Other New England States* (Vol. I, 1925) by Edward Howe Forbush, Fuertes contributed, over the years, paintings of many hundreds of birds. From 1904 to 1927 he also painted and drew for almost every issue of *Bird-Lore,* which Chapman edited; for other professional magazines; and for more than sixty books. He had lesser commissions of the same sort and painted many individual pictures for private persons as well as a famous series of twenty-four oils for the Frederick F. Brewster home in New Haven, Connecticut, a commission he received through Dr. Sanford. Many people turned to him for sketches or paintings to use as presents. "I find it very hard," he said, "even at my busiest times, to refuse little things that require almost as much thought and planning as big ones, so I never get a time when I can really let up."[17] His commissions crowded him. "How," he once complained to Chapman, "shall I tote this hot-weather nightmare?" He had sent off, he said, "your ten chewink plates. I wish I could have achieved it earlier. Beck's Pheasants have had a long rest and worry me. I have 30 small color plates to do for Henshaw and the 4 last State [*Birds of New York*] Plates —all yapping still."[18] This was close to the normal state of his work. Only once did the flow of work seem likely to dwindle: that was early in World War I when pictures of birds were in little demand. The National Geographic Society put him back in action by calling for a series of portraits of dogs. He was soon hard at work and spoke of himself as "busy's 'ell painting, for God's sake, dogs."[19]

In professional matters Fuertes' demands were modest, but he certainly stood on his rights in dealing with ordinary commercial publishers and would not make cut-rate agreements. "I have no means of support but my work, which I have spent much time and labor and study in perfecting and I do not hesitate a moment to put that fact before the publishers."[20] However, he asked no more than about $15 to $25 for color plates and somewhere between $125 and $250 for his larger pictures. And these prices he modified to suit the purse of, for instance, a secretary who had told one of Fuertes' friends that she would love to own a picture by Mr. Fuertes.

Common Crow
Corvus brachyrhynchos
North America
Wash drawing
approximately 5½" x 7¼"

Although Fuertes resisted some tempting expedition offers from Chapman, he did take more modest trips to keep his wanderlust somewhat satisfied. In addition to his lectures and professional meetings, he returned to the Bahamas in 1913, where he first used a motion-picture camera as an aid, and in 1920 went to Florida again. During the summer of 1924 he accepted an invitation to the Netherlands from Hendrik van Loon, who for a while had rented half of Fuertes' two-family house in Ithaca, and in 1925 his daughter Mary enthusiastically accompanied him to Wyoming. In 1923, at the repeated urging of President Livingston Farrand of Cornell, Fuertes became a resident lecturer at the university, his only formal academic connection. Again, a steady stream of illustrations and plates, paintings and drawings, flowed from his crowded studio. He even did some cards for Church & Dwight to be enclosed in Arm and Hammer baking-soda packages.

On the trip to Wyoming, Fuertes, as usual, met and befriended a man who was eager to undertake a truly exotic and lavish trip with him. James E. Baum, a sportsman and journalist, decided that for hunting, collecting, and just plain public curiosity Ethiopia was the ideal place for an expedition. By the time he finished his arrangements, they included underwriting from the Field Museum of Natural History in Chicago and the *Chicago Daily News*. Not since the Harriman days had Fuertes traveled in such style. Wilfred Hudson Osgood, curator of zoology at the museum and an old friend of Fuertes, also went along, and in addition to collecting, exploring the countryside, studying the customs of a strange country,

and painting, the party also was received and entertained by Haile Selassie, then regent of Ethiopia. It was in all ways a rich trip, and Fuertes' letters record his enthusiasm for every aspect of it.

After picking up his wife and daughter, who were touring in Britain, Fuertes returned to the United States, hoping to finish his contracted work and get down to work for himself. With his Ethiopia pictures in hand, Fuertes and his wife paid a visit to the Chapmans in August, 1927. On the return trip, on August 22, Fuertes, trying to pass a haywagon, was instantly killed when he drove his car onto a grade crossing and was struck by a passing train. His wife was seriously injured, but the pictures were thrown to safety. Fuertes was privately buried on August 25.

Fuertes' legacy was rich. He left many friends, some who had known him throughout his life, others who had met him briefly but remembered him vividly. It is Fuertes' artistic work, however, that is his most enduring testimony. Fuertes' overwhelming interest was birds, and to this passion he brought his powers of observation and his capacity for sustained, concentrated effort. To understand these qualities is to understand Fuertes' productive and successful career as ornithologist, illustrator, and ultimately as artist.

Fuertes was an active field ornithologist who spent much of his life in jungles, forests, and mountains in search of birds. He studied the geographical distribution of different species of birds, found new species—one was named after him—observed habits, hunted specimens, and prepared skins for his own collection and museum collections. Over his life Fuertes also amassed an immense knowledge of birds and bird

Northern Shrike
Lanius excubitor
Holarctic
Wash drawing
approximately 5" x 5"

anatomy. Tireless in his study and drawing, at mid-career he could say with truth, "I have been longer a student of the comparative anatomy, appearance, and general 'personal looks' of the birds themselves, and have spent a larger proportion of my time since boyhood in the direct study of birds, and have seen more widely varied types in life, than almost anyone I know."[21]

Fuertes' techniques in the field are interesting in themselves, aside from their importance as the basis for his illustrative and artistic careers.

When he was on an expedition, Fuertes usually spent the first part of his day, from daybreak until noon, in hunting. After lunch he skinned and prepared the birds he had collected. Skinning and preparing took four or five hours, and Fuertes then turned to painting. After work he compiled his journal and wrote letters.

As a field ornithologist Fuertes had one interesting specialty in which he was perhaps unique, his knowledge of bird songs and his ability to reproduce them. He had an ear for music and an excellent memory, and his imitations were exact. Again and again he used this skill—at least one of his discoveries of a new bird came from recognizing and reproducing a new song —to call birds to him. He would then shoot his prize, sketch it, and add it to the expedition's collection.

Fuertes' records are complete and exact, a carry-over from his boyhood notations. The records of his fieldwork in Texas in 1901, for example, are still important in the study of birds in Texas. His journal minutely describes the new birds he saw; each species is listed, with the date and time of day when seen, the

exact hillside or ravine, the sex of the bird, and what it was doing. Sometimes the notes even say whether the bird was carrying food in its mouth. Fuertes also made sketches of individual birds, most often of parts, notably the head, the neck, and the feet. This was, so to speak, for the record, the portrayal of an individual specimen which would later serve as reference material in his studio, when he would also be working with a number of skins before him to paint a picture of the species. Almost all the pictures reproduced in this book are of individual birds he painted in the field or immediately after his return to the studio. He wished to record in these sketches the precise range of color of the parts of the bird he would be painting, and thus he took elaborate pencil notes to describe down to the last detail the color he would wish to recapture. In one of his sketches he concentrated on the tone of the inside of a baby bird's mouth. In pencil he drew a vivid sketch of the bird, its mouth partly open. He painted only the inside of the mouth, using a rich red. But that was not enough; alongside he added, "Mouth semi transparent, like a yew-berry."

Wherever he was, Fuertes covered with drawings all kinds of scraps of paper, back and front; occasionally he used a bill, or even wrapping paper if nothing else were handy. His sketches show his constant studying of birds, looking at them from different angles, in different modes of flight, in different poses, the head turned this way or that, the body bent forward or reaching upward. He worked especially hard at the difficult positions, the head-on shots of the bird flying toward him or the front-face view of the head itself. His desire to get things exactly right sometimes

Red-tailed Hawk
Buteo jamaicensis
North America
Pencil drawing
approximately 6" x 9"

led him to take a second look not only at the bird but at its prey. His notes show that after he drew a hawk with a dead mouse he made another try at the head of the mouse to make sure that it looked convincingly dead. Among Fuertes' papers is one small envelope containing a dozen or so cutouts of some drawings of a wild turkey. Each shows the bird in a different position, each is from a different angle; presumably he had been at work on a larger picture and wished to satisfy himself that, when he painted that picture, he would place the turkey in the best possible manner to suit the total composition.

Fuertes made field sketches because "opportunities come very rarely for making life drawings with the aid of a field-glass, but by far the largest part of the field drawings are made from freshly shot birds. Little sketch studies for attitudes are made in numbers whenever it is possible, but work in the field is seldom finished in detail beyond the very careful representation of the real appearance of the parts that have fugitive color or form and the very rare cases in which the colors of the feathers themselves change after the death of their wearers." He spoke of the "bloomy" gray of some hawks, doves, and herons, "which like a delicate powder rubs off the feathers and leaves a dead, dark undercolor." This powder he likened to the bloom sometimes seen on grapes.[22]

But these on-the-spot sketches and notes were not his only resource. Fuertes also had an extraordinary memory. Osgood recalled "being with Fuertes when, in Glen Alpine near Lake Tahoe, he for the first time saw a living dipper. The bird's distinctive form, poses, and gestures entranced him as he watched it through his binoculars, but not a single sketch was made. Nevertheless, later, when describing the experience, sketches showing the bird's characteristic actions rolled from his pencil as readily as though the bird were still before him."[23] Frank Chapman said, "His mind appears to be a delicately sensitized plate designed especially to catch and fix images of bird life. And of such images he filed and had at his finger tips for use a countless number, for his opportunities for field study have been greater than those of any other painter of birds."[24]

These records, sketches, and memories were, of course, only the basis of Fuertes' main occupation—illustration. The master of his craft for a generation, he designed and drew bird plates from the age of twenty-two on. These he painted in either wash or water color.

His book illustrations had in almost all instances a single purpose: "to make the subject as characteristic in appearance and recognizable in its detail as possible."[25] When he designed and painted a plate, with perhaps a male, female, and immature member of a species, he made the birds stand out clearly and boldly against a minimum of landscape or background. He put into his portrait all the elements of color, form, and attitude that were characteristic of the species. To paint a song sparrow, he would study individuals by the dozen and then select the elements he judged to be the common characteristics. Hence his continuous work in the field and borrowing of bird skins.

George Miksch Sutton, an illustrator of birds who at fifteen began a correspondence with Fuertes, gives a wonderful picture of Fuertes at work:

Steller's Jay
Cyanocitta stelleri
Western North America
Wash drawing
approximately 5½″ x 7″

There sat Fuertes—a dried bird-skin in his left hand, a spray of wild morning-glory before him in a little vase, a piece of paper thumbtacked to an old drawing board in front of him—and the phoebe came to life before my very eyes. He held the phoebe skin while he worked, turning it this way and that, looking at it closely, counting its feathers with his pencil, blowing at it to make it fluffy, going to the window once or twice to examine its gape or eye-lid or rictal bristles in a stronger light. The specimen had been prepared in a special way—loosely stuffed; the head at a life-like, even a jaunty angle; the feet sticking out or up, rather than lying flat as in approved cabinet specimens. He worked rapidly, putting down pencil stroke after pencil stroke without pause. Then he laid the phoebe skin aside, held the drawing at arm's length, took up his eraser, and rubbed the whole thing out. The bird wasn't placed right. He started again.[26]

A great deal of Fuertes' work was done for Frank Chapman. Although Chapman and Fuertes were close friends, regarding each other with respect and affection, it was the painting Fuertes did for Chapman that kept them in close association over the years. For the habitat displays at the American Museum, for the semipopular ornithological magazine *Bird-Lore,* of which he was the editor, and for his renowned *Handbook of the Birds of the Eastern United States,* Chapman needed many pictures of birds. As the author, Chapman described what he wished to have portrayed—what species of birds; what particular individual—male, female, adult, immature; in breeding or fall plumage; what variations. Fuertes, the artist, put the birds on paper. When Fuertes' own field notes, sketches, and bird skins were sufficient, which they usually were, he went ahead. When they were not, Chapman sent up skins from the American Museum.

As a rule, Chapman, a hard man to satisfy, was highly pleased with what he got. When he was not, there began a frank exchange of views such as only the best professionals can manage in good spirit. After receiving a group of plates, Chapman wrote, "With the tanagers success is not apparent," and added, more strongly, "I have to confess that I am really terribly disappointed to find that you have not made the fly-catcher plate like the thrush plate."[27] Fuertes replied,

Yesterday's letter, as might have been expected, shot a bolt into my insides. I must confess, myself, to liking the tanager plate the least. It hung fire a long time, and while it never quite satisfied me it was plain in showing what I conceived to be the requirements of the plate, and is in many ways the most difficult of the lot. The reds have all to be built up, at intervals of several days, of different colors: Chinese white (which is subdeliquescent, and takes sometimes a week to dry out), then an accurate covering of yellow which must not "pull up" the white, another settling for a day or two, then lastly a graded and modeled dressing for the final red, which may not be touched subsequently and which must not drag up the willing under-colors. That's the only way *I* can get even a *fairly* brilliant scarlet, and it's *some* job, especially when it's mixed and varied with dull olive and yellows, which with the slightest overlapping make a *black* line. Send it back, and I'll do what I can—radical changes are impossible, except doing it all over new. . . . I was genuinely disappointed that you didn't like the flycatcher plate. . . . I thought that one of the prettiest little compositions of the lot.[28]

In general, Fuertes was ready, for the sake of improving emphasis or making a composition clearer, to heighten color or to rearrange figures. He drew the line only at making alterations that would go against what his own observations told him. To Chapman's criticism of a drawing he replied, "The wren-tit's tail was purposely twitched, but I can easily make it less obvious. I jerked it a bit for two reasons—*one,* to show the gradation of feathers and *two* (to justify one) the

Wren Tit
Chamaea fasciata
North America west of Sierra Nevada
Wash drawing
approximately 5½" x 4½"

Magnolia Warbler
Dendroica magnolia
North America
Wash drawing
approximately 2½" x 2½"

fact that he's momentarily stuck up, tilt-wise, on the twig and his tail is helping to hold him for the instant before he jumps down into the brush again."[29] To another criticism he said, "The hawk is all right. I have watched practically all *genera* shown, and all do as I have shown *accipiter,* i.e. carry the prey at almost leg-length and slightly back. Sparrow-hawks carry mice that way. Ospreys invariably carry fish [so]. Roughlegs carry even small field mice that way, and peregrines, doves. This I am as sure of as that they use their wings in flying, and repeatedly observed it. In all cases I have ever seen of a hawk or eagle carrying prey it has always been carried well away from the body."[30]

Illustration was Fuertes' profession, and an activity to which he devoted a great portion of his time and from which he gained a great portion of his financial support. His work, however, went beyond the confines of simply preparing illustrative materials. Fuertes' plates were suffused with his creative art, and it was to the calling of artist that he dedicated his rich and natural abilities, his highly skilled powers of observation, and his bold and energetic spirit.

It was not a career without its difficulties. Fuertes once succinctly summed it up: "Hell to be an artist and have work, but Heller not to, I suppose,"[31] though in a more quiet mood he said of himself, "a busy man, occupied with the work he most loves, has little time or reason for bemoaning his fate."[32] The huge number of his assignments and the rigorous pace they demanded often left Fuertes little time to do his own work in his own way. His daughter recalls his artistic dilemma, which in part turned around the back-

grounds against which Fuertes painted his birds. For illustrative work, it was vitally important that the bird stand out sharply and clearly. Yet Fuertes was an early convert to Abbott Thayer's theories of concealing coloration (natural camouflage), and he was extremely vulnerable to the criticisms of Thayer, who was not only his teacher but his great friend. By way of explanation Fuertes wrote to Thayer and painfully spelled out the situation: "I can imagine no more luxurious activity than to paint every little creature we have beautifully availing himself of his many devices for obliteration (short of hiding) . . . instead of the much less thrilling representation—as I feel I have to do—of their specific superficial appearance detached at least in part from their merging environment."[33]

Louis Agassiz Fuertes, for most of his professional life, had little time for luxuries, but he was deeply aware of his artistic mission and pursued it seriously.

Perhaps the quality that most immediately draws the viewer to Fuertes' work is its intensity. Fuertes literally tried to *feel* a bird and to re-create this emotional impact directly on paper. As a painter, Fuertes was at first all eyes as he strained to encompass a new bird. Chapman's description of him at work conveys the feeling with full force: "Fuertes in possession of a freshly captured specimen of a bird which was before unknown to him, is for the time wholly beyond the reach of all sensations other than those occasioned by the specimen before him. His concentration annihilates his surroundings. Color, pattern, form, contour, minute details of structure, all absorbed and assimilated so completely that they become part of himself,

L. A. Fuertes.

and they can be reproduced at any future time with amazing accuracy."[34]

Largely self-taught, Fuertes did not regard his gift of observation and re-creation as given by the gods. He worked hard at his art, and throughout his letters to his friends and advice to younger artists there are references to his study, to his training himself, to the thought and effort that went into the paintings and drawings that seemed to flow so easily from his hand. To young painters who approached him for advice Fuertes always stressed study, and the hard, continued apprenticeship of the young professional. There were no short cuts, he said, no mysteries. Above all, the student who wished to be a skillful painter of nature must know his subject. "The one fundamental, basic prerequisite of all art, particularly naturalistic art," he believed, "must be good, sound, deep, and appreciative knowledge."[35] Further, the great nature painters were men who studied "the actual local color of objects and elements, the effect and direction of the light bathing these elements and the color reflected from lighted parts onto shaded parts." Those things the student was not to "behold" or "observe" or "look at" but to "see" to the full extent of his "visual capacity." Having seen them, he must "work without stint" to put them on paper or canvas.[36]

Thus, at the root of Fuertes' art was solid knowledge and a hard-won appreciation of the labor of art. But, of course, no art as vital as Fuertes' can be based purely on knowledge, practice, and study. Most fundamental to Fuertes' work is his never-ceasing excitement at the world he beheld. "Pure beauty in all things fascinated him," remarked Osgood; "the exquisite combinations of color and texture exhibited by many small birds were his constant joy. But it is significant that his favorites among all birds were falcons, the swiftest, boldest, most dashing, and, withal, the most rapacious and inexorably bloodthirsty of their kind."[37] It is this love for the vigor, even the violence, of nature that informs Fuertes' best work. Fuertes was occupied with the business of life. His own rich and warm personality embraced it, and his art affirms this deeply held vision of the world.

Fuertes' achievements as a painter of birds called forth, even when he was young, a comparison with the work of Audubon. Audubon was the greatest American painter of birds and a highly knowledgeable naturalist. In the days of the American frontier, two generations before Fuertes, he created in his *Birds of America* a work that was almost unbelievable in its accuracy, scope, and romantic spirit. His pioneer work in identifying birds and painting them deserved and still claims the highest admiration.

Where Fuertes differed from Audubon was in his photographic memory and his ability to convey with brush and pencil the impression of a living bird. Like Fuertes, Audubon often made his sketches from the bird he had just shot. "A recently killed bird was fixed in the position desired by means of wires and placed against a background ruled with division lines in squares to correspond with similar lines in Audubon's paper."[38] As his pictures show, Audubon wished to get away from the wooden poses in which his predecessors presented birds; accordingly, he often tried to depict dramatic action—perhaps a bird striding forward or pursuing an insect or one bird reared up

Sage Grouse
Centrocercus urophasianus
Western North America
Pencil drawing
approximately 7" x 13"

against another, beak open, wings fully extended. Audubon's plates are full of action, and the total composition as seen in the finished engravings is totally pleasing. But the plates and the water colors show that Audubon, in striving for dramatic effect, sometimes gave up part of the reality of the life of the bird itself and substituted for it a colorful figure. In Fuertes' field sketches and drawings the bird is truly alive.

What Fuertes painted was the "personal look," as he called it, of the living bird—what it looked like when its whole body, especially its eyes, conveyed the force of life. This was his great gift, which Thayer spotted in Fuertes from the beginning. "You are extraordinary in the intimate way you represent them," said Thayer; he saw "so much revelation of the secret of each bird's personal appearance."[39] Most of the paintings and drawings reproduced in this book are studies of individual birds, each seen as a singular living creature. No other painter of birds has equaled them.

Fuertes was a productive artist for thirty years, during which he produced thousands of drawings and paintings. His passionate interest in birds was there from childhood. By the time he was twenty he was a skillful painter of birds, and throughout his life he enlarged his knowledge of birds and art almost continuously. He had, he said, a single purpose as an artist —to paint a portrait of the living thing as he saw it or, in his words, "to discover and crystallize truth into visible and permanent form."[40] This is the task to which Louis Agassiz Fuertes devoted his life's work, and he left a record of splendid achievement. But he put more than his love of nature and artistic skill into his finest paintings. He devoted his immense energy to the task of capturing, through his own heightened sensitivities, the spirit of birds. As Frank Chapman said in his eulogy, "If the birds of the world had met to select a human being who could best express to mankind the beauty and charm of their forms, their songs, their rhythmic flight, their manners for the heart's delight, they would unquestionably have chosen Louis Fuertes."[41]

NOTES

1. L.A.F. to Frank Chapman, December 25, 1917. "This set was for ten years or more my daily bread. By it I was so thrilled that it melts me now to remember it."

2. L.A.F. to Frank Chapman, January 7, 1911.

3. Frank Chapman. "In Memoriam, L.A.F.," *The Auk*, Vol. XLV (January, 1928), p. 2.

4. *Ibid.*, p. 3.

5. L.A.F. to Frank H. Herrick, February 7, 1918.

6. The exhibit took place at Rothschild's Store in Ithaca, New York, about 1892. I was told this story by Miss Mary Hull, sister of a colleague of mine at Cornell. She was the lady who spoke with young Louis.

7. Mary Fuertes Boynton, *Louis Agassiz Fuertes*. New York. Oxford University Press, 1956, p. 6.

Green Heron
Butorides virescens
North America, Northern South America
Pencil drawing
approximately 3" x 2"

8. Abbott H. Thayer to L.A.F., December 25, 1896.

9. Thayer to L.A.F., March 24, 1897.

10. Thayer to L.A.F., May 11, 1897.

11. Thayer to L.A.F., May 9, 1897.

12. Mary Fuertes Boynton, *op. cit.*, p. 18.

13. *Ibid.*, pp. 82–83.

14. L.A.F. to Margaret Sumner Fuertes, January 6, 1913.

15. L.A.F. to Frank Chapman, May 18, 1909.

16. Mary Fuertes Boynton, *op. cit.*, p. 259.

17. L.A.F. to Isaac F. Roberts, November 7, 1911.

18. L.A.F. to Frank Chapman, June 29, 1912.

19. L.A.F. to Wilfred H. Osgood, March 20, 1918.

20. L.A.F. to Frank Chapman, August 17, 1911.

21. L.A.F., draft of letter to W. Leon Dawson, September, 1916.

22. The quotations in this paragraph are all from an article in *The Amateur Sportsman*, Vol. XLII, No. 5 (September, 1910). The article is unsigned, but Fuertes' records make it clear that he was the author.

23. Frank Chapman, quoting Wilfred H. Osgood in "Fuertes and Audubon," *Natural History*, March, 1937, p. 207.

24. Frank Chapman, "Louis Agassiz Fuertes, 1874–1927," obituary in *Bird-Lore*, September–October, 1927, p. 361.

25. L.A.F. to Dr. Albert K. Fisher, August 19, 1915.

26. George Miksch Sutton, "Louis Fuertes, Teacher," an install-ment of Sutton's regular column, "The Wildlife Gallery," *The Audubon Magazine*, January–February, 1942, p. 521.

27. Frank Chapman to L.A.F., November 22, 1911.

28. L.A.F. to Chapman, November 24, 1911.

29. L.A.F. to Chapman, November 25, 1915.

30. L.A.F. to Chapman, December 29, 1911.

31. L.A.F. to Chapman, December 17, 1915.

32. L.A.F. to Isaac F. Roberts, April 7, 1911.

33. L.A.F. to Abbott H. Thayer, March 3, 1917.

34. "Louis Agassiz Fuertes, 1874–1927," obituary in *Bird-Lore*, *op. cit.*

35. L.A.F. to Conrad Roland, September 15, 1925.

36. L.A.F. to Keith Williams, no date; between May 26, 1921, and December 4, 1922.

37. Wilfred H. Osgood, "Introduction" in L.A.F.'s *An Album of Abyssinian Birds and Mammals*. Chicago: Field Museum of Natural History, 1930, p. 1.

38. Francis Hobart Herrick, *Audubon the Naturalist*. New York: Appleton, 1917. Vol. I, p. 183.

39. Abbott H. Thayer to L.A.F., May 3, 1898.

40. L.A.F. to Conrad Roland, September 15, 1925.

41. The speech was given by Chapman at a memorial service for Fuertes in Ithaca on October 30, 1927. It was reprinted in the *Cornell Alumni News*, Vol. XXX. (1927), p. 84.

THE LETTERS

The letters excerpted here are the record of six of Louis Agassiz Fuertes' major expeditions—the Harriman expedition to Alaska in 1899, the U.S. Biological Survey expedition to Texas in 1901, The American Museum of Natural History expedition to Mexico in 1910, the American Museum expedition to Colombia in 1911, the second American Museum Colombia expedition in 1913, and the Field Museum of Natural History–Chicago Daily News expedition to Abyssinia in 1926–1927.

Fuertes wrote his travel letters quite consciously as a means of keeping a record and of placing "as much as possible of what has come my way before the homefolks' imagination." When he could do so, he put the record together day by day, compiling something like a journal which at the end of a week or so he would send by messenger to the nearest town or drop off at a port or river station. He wrote most of these letters from the jungle or desert or mountainside, usually after a hard day's work, and by the light of a candle or "taller [tallow] dip."

In these letters Fuertes the naturalist and the artist is revealed remarkably. His utterly scientific and unsentimental methods—he admitted to being embarrassed by gushing nature lovers—and his continuing awe are the outstanding qualities of the letters, but they are of much more than personal importance.

In the early days of the great modern museums, the rigorous expeditions undertaken by men like Vernon Bailey, Frank Chapman, Wilfred Hudson Osgood, Fuertes, and others supplied invaluable data and specimens. On the journeys Fuertes usually had as professional companions three or four ornithologists and zoologists. Together the scientists organized their expeditions to mountainside or jungle, set up camp, and then each morning went their separate ways, sometimes accompanied by native guides. As a result of their zeal, the great American natural history museums were able to expand their collections with innumerable animal skins and other materials, and to assemble the lifelike displays for which they became famous. The painstaking accuracy of the exhibits relied greatly on the powers of observation and on the memories of the field naturalists, especially in the period before the camera came into wide use. Fuertes and his companions also brought to a growing, eager public knowledge of distant and unfamiliar places. Their own interest in the places they visited and the people they met is another striking feature of this correspondence.

Harriman Alaska Expedition, 1899

In 1899, Fuertes joined the Harriman Alaska expedition on the recommendation of Dr. C. Hart Merriam, chief of the U.S. Biological Survey (later the U.S. Fish and Wildlife Service). E. H. Harriman, the railroad magnate and financier, planned a journey by sea to Alaska for his family and a few friends. For them the journey was to be an opportunity to relax aboard ship and to see the scenery, the people at the ports where they put in, and the wildlife. Harriman chartered the S.S. George W. Elder, *a vessel so large that he decided to invite, in addition to his own group of intimates, some scientists, so that the expedition might leave a scientific record as well as a collection of materials—minerals, marine life, animals, plants. From Merriam, Harriman received a list of twenty-five distinguished scientists, including the nature writer John Burroughs and three artists, of whom one was Fuertes. The voyage covered 4,327 miles and lasted from June 1 to August 1, 1899. The ship's total company was 126.*

On this expedition Fuertes made associations that were of considerable importance to him later. Merriam became the father-in-law of Vernon Bailey, an eminent zoologist and long-time friend of Fuertes. Ned Trudeau, a young doctor who was practicing at Saranac Lake, N.Y., became a well-known specialist in the treatment of tuberculosis. "Young Osgood"— Wilfred H. Osgood—also a lifelong friend of Fuertes, and later curator of zoology at the Field Museum of Natural History, accompanied Fuertes on the expedition to Abyssinia in 1926–27.

The letters in this group were written to his parents on pads of eight or ten pages each. Fuertes called them "a bunch of notes." He made up a letter by adding a page or two of writing whenever he had a chance, closing each letter when he had an opportunity to mail it. He also kept a journal with more specific information regarding the birds he saw and collected.

Near Granger, Wyo., May [26?], 1899
. . . We began the day practically at Cheyenne, Wyoming, at 7 a.m. Long before that, however, I'd heard my first Western meadow lark and the black and white lark bunting was to be seen often. . . .

May 28
. . . The Sawtooth mountains were behind us and some other snow peaks way ahead—and in the sage were jack-rabbits and small mammals, while Western meadow larks, shore larks, lark finches, and various sparrows were to be heard and seen all the time. Also the yellow ground and faint, downy green sagebrush were sprinkled thickly with bright patches of yellow, crimson and bright blue flowers—sunflowers, forget-menots, paint brush, phlox, blue larkspur and various flowering lily-like plants and grasses. . . .

When we got home [from a visit to Shoshone Falls], some two or three of the party had returned from a short trip up the track and brought back a big basket of Rocky Mt. brook trout, from 8 inches to about 14, which we had for supper and did justice to. We all turned in rather early. I was the last as I'd had to write the day's birdnotes up before I forgot them. . . .

As I sit here in the car window, writing, the yellow

Black-billed Magpie
Pica pica
Holarctic
Wash drawing
approximately 7½" x 5"

Foot of Common Gallinule
Gallinula chloropus
Almost worldwide
Wash drawing
approximately 4½" x 5½"

warblers and western robins sing exactly as they do in the trees by our house—and Bullock's oriole, the Arkansas flycatcher and crimson-fronted finches recall eastern relatives, but have a decidedly foreign accent. The meadowlarks you would never know, as they sound like a mixture of bobolink and woodthrush, with the accent on the latter, done in a clear flutey starling quality. . . .

May 30

I'll stop this part of the account now and finish up and send it off from Seattle, just before going aboard. . . . Ned Trudeau, a young fellow along, Dr. Morris's "assistant," has volunteered to help me skin birds and the younger Miss Harriman and a Miss Averell, her cousin from Rochester . . . are assistant artists whom we *real things* can call upon to help us in press of work. . . .

[On board the Steamer George W. Elder, *a few hours out of Seattle.]*

June 1

. . . The sea has been like a lake all day and we had a most wonderful sunset, in which snow mountains, and immense ones, were in the foreground and wonderful purple Mts. and hills vanished in their lavender over the horizon, and an orange sky, with crude blood edged purple clouds met a glowing ocean, running cold, light blue behind us, and all the indescribable colors that attend such a thing as an ocean sunset were lavishly plashed in.

I've got the finest studio in the bunch—right up in the skylights over the engine room—a place painted white with a course of windows all around and skylights overhead—all alone, 'cause I thought of it and pushed it through (with Miss Harriman's suggestion and help) . . . .

[The ship had put in at Lou's Inlet, Grenville Channel, British Columbia.]

June 3

. . . I struck right into the forest along the left shore, and found it next to impenetrable. It had been raining and the brush was wet, and the logs, which were almost the only highway, very slippery. I had one quite bad tumble, but it didn't do any damage beyond a red pancake mark on the slats—and a jolt in the wind. I heard a pileolated warbler, and after an hour's search within a few yards of it, through the deep brush, and all within a radius of 100 feet, I finally got a glance at it, as it disappeared over a mossy boulder into the ferns beyond. Saw a creeper go into its nest on the side of a dead spruce tree, and saw some more rufous hummers—the strangest thing to see a bright foxcolored hummingbird s-s-sing like a creeper, with a big bumble-bee buzz—curve up into a giant forest, where everything in view is vast; pose with its tail, pendulum-like, swinging under it, look around, and brooooooom off again, all before you quite notice it! Or to hear a little undertone hum, look up, and see through the leaves of a red-flowered blackberry bush a tiny white-throated female looking at you solicitously for a scared second, and quietly fade away.

Louis Agassiz Fuertes

Fulvous Tree Duck
Dendrocygna bicolor
South and West United States,
Mexico, South
America, East Africa,
Madagascar, India, Ceylon
Pencil drawing
approximately 6½" x 3¾"

I had been hearing the most curious and loud noises up in the forest, and started toward them, when they got so queer and human sounding that I thought that Dr. Fisher, who is summat of a jollier, was doing it to get a rise out of me. So I got proud, and turned off. When we got back to the ship, after hearing a shot or two, Dr. Fisher appeared with a great big northern raven, which I have made some right careful drawings of. . . .

June 4

. . . I seem to find ravens and rufous hummingbirds always together. The latter were so common that almost every proper "spitz" had its little red ball on top, and the ravens were astonishingly common and allowed one to get very near—within 40 or 50 feet.

June 5

The scenery is so much more magnificent than anything I have ever seen that I can't begin on it anywhere. Now we will be sailing in a narrow channel, with great wooded hills rising straight out of the water —now the passage will open out and we will be in a channel miles wide with rounded, ice-cut hills lining the shores—beyond these in a complete circle great saw edged ragged ranges of snow mountains—hundreds of miles of Matterhorns, some of them very columns, thousands of feet high. Immense snowfields and glaciers show themselves in the hollows between peaks and the coloring of everything is too rich to be believable.

No one here has ever seen such vegetation as fills the woods—one can go all around in them without setting his foot on the ground once in ten steps, by walking the fallen logs—from no distance at all to ten or fifteen feet above the ground. The sphagnum and other mosses are feet thick, and a rich green under-glow suffuses everything—and the great majestic spruce columns—often eight or even more feet in diameter, and as much as 200 feet high, gray where not clothed in some bright green or yellow moss—and the immense stillness broken only by a hummer's squeak or a raven's great raucous yells, make a combination which it is a little beyond my power to describe. . . .

June 7, 10 P.M.

This has been about the most curious and delightful day we've had yet. Early we had breakfast and got things together to take the narrow gauge train up to White Pass. The town has long log-cabin suburbs, and the line passes through this settlement and follows the Skagway river up to the summit, nearly 3000 feet up. The day was drizzly, and we were in clouds most of the way—20 miles of climb. We got out and looked around every little while, and when nearly up to the big curve, two-thirds of the way up, Dr. M. suddenly jumped up, saying, "Well, there are some of my boys!" And the train stopped, and backed a little distance, and sure enough, there was a little outfit, with three men, one of whom was Osgood, a young fellow I knew in Washington very well, collecting mammals and birds. It was a joy to see him, and he seemed glad to

24

Horned Grebe
Podiceps auritus
Holarctic
Wash drawing
approximately 2½" x 3½"

see me, even with all the others he knew of the party. He came with us to the summit.

It is known as "Dead Horse Trail," and gets its name from the fact that year before last, over 3000 horses and 26 men died in going over it.

The trail from Summit over to the Yukon 675 miles, is paved, to use a miners' expression, with horse-bones. We saw three dead ones in a short ¼ mile. . . .

As soon as we stopped . . . I struck up the side of the hill, in the snow and scrubby fir. The ground is all granite rock and boulders, dense and deep in mosses and lichens, with thick, tough, flatly-growing spruces, as high, in some places, as three feet, generally one half of that. . . . Ridgway was also near me, and soon I heard a sweet clear sparrow song, which I guessed to be that of the lovely golden-crowned sparrow, a bird like our eastern white-crown . . . with a golden yellow crown. . . . Pop! went Ridgway's auxiliary, and the bird came my way, and lit above me over a ledge. I climbed excitedly up to it, and it looked up, nearer than I thought, for when I shot it with a pinch I ruined it. I was very sick, but got another, a beauty, in a few more minutes. . . .

When we got back to the station [at Summit] we were all told to gather in the "Hotel"—a big double tent—for lunch. We all went in, ate everything off of one granite plate, and had about the best lunch we've had yet, and that's saying a lot. I painted the birds we got from 5 to 7, ate dinner and painted again till 9; then sang a bit with Fernow, chased around the deck a dozen or so times to keep my hand in, and then came down here to write up this log. . . .

I am sending you things that have come my way and may interest you, as showing the curious activity man has in these queer regions. It is rather repulsive and unpleasant, the atmosphere created by the gold seekers up here—you see signs of awful cruelty to horses—selfish hustling, "devil take everybody else" sort of attitude, and are made rather sick by the gold hungry look on the faces of men, packs on their backs, that you see plodding the trails for the Klondike. I guess many a serious thought has faced those fellows when they were tired—struck a bunch of skeletons or a deserted pack or outfit—but they seem to keep on.

Your affectionate,
Louis

Before Muir Glacier, Glacier Bay, June 8
This morning I awoke and looked out of my portholes and was astonished not to see anything but blue and it turned out that I was looking into the wall face of a big iceberg about 15 feet from the ship's side.

Dr. Fisher and I went ashore with our guns . . . and headed down beach toward a big alder covered face of the rock where Rocky Mt. goats had been seen a day or two before. We weren't after goats, but it looked like a fine collecting ground. We are too near the glacier for any but a few birds. We had gone about ¼ mile when I spied a flock of ducks down close to the shore. So I left Fisher and "crawled on to 'em," until about 100 yards from shore I had to stomach it. I was rewarded though, for when I shot into the flock I killed three magnificent Harlequin ducks (Merriam and Elliott are the only ones aboard who have ever seen them alive before).

While I was at work in my studio over the engines,

25

Burrowing Owl
Speotyto cunicularia
Western North America
Pencil drawing
approximately 8" x 5"

I heard the old glacier booming and roaring and tore out in time to see the most majestic of sights. Great combers and promontories of ice were falling off, and the deep rumbling thunder of its parting, the seething roar of the water . . . [were grand enough, as was the] sight of the great pieces, some of them 300 feet long, tottering forward, and sending first a towering fountain of snowy foam and spray clear over the glacier top, then an immense, dark wave that would set all the bergs moving, go crashing to shore where it would pike and tower between the stranded ice boulders, and roll in roaring surf along the shore, and finally reach us and give us a long deep roll. But the most majestic thing of all was the rising of the fallen mass. After the big 20 or 30 foot wave, the water would seem to be quiet, then dome up close to the glacier face a clear light blue vault, which would rise—rise—and finally break to let out the great ice mass, and recede from its apex in seething streams. The great thing would rise, rocking from side to side, until it was as high as the glacier top, and then slowly subside, and float silently away from its bed for the past thousands or so of years. . . .

June 10, night

Dr. Fernow, Dr. Fisher, Robert Ridgway, Kearny and I and Cole are in camp, at last, on Gustavus point. We got in about noon, made camp, got lunch and went out. It is a most ideal spot, the woods are most beautiful, deep in soft moss, so that one makes no sound in going through them, and the trunks are covered with light blue-gray mosses and lichens, so that the colors are soft and harmonious. I got a number of birds, and did a good bit of collecting in the nest, eggs, and parent birds of the lovely lutescent warbler. The dwarf hermit thrushes are making most lovely harmony in the woods on all sides of this clearing, and the crackling campfire and Dr. Fernow's Franco-Prussian war stories make it very nice to be here. But though I'm writing in broad daylight, and have made two drawings since supper, it is after 10, and we want to make an early start, so I'm going to bed—adios.

Sunday, June 11

. . . We are in a cove between two rocky and sandy points, with fine spruce forests behind us, the long blue bay in front; we can't see out to sea on any side, but the deep blue is cut by white or light blue ice cakes floating on the tide, some near enough to show their queer fantastic shapes. Three or four whales are sporting around in the bay, snorting, lunging out of the water and landing with a big splash, or just curving up and under, giving a final swash with their tails.

There has been a bird note which has mystified us all. We all heard it yesterday, and determined to ferret it out this morning, and I was the lucky man. The note came from deep in the woods, was very loud, pure, and beautiful, the quality of a veery's call note, only intensely pure and loud. It was absolutely a monotone, as true as a flute, beginning *piano* and going through a fine *crescendo,* and dying out again at the end. First it would be given in a fine soprano, and after a few seconds it would come in a deep contralto; the third would perhaps be between the two in pitch,

Bare-legged Owl
Gymnoglaux lawrencii
Cuba, Isle of Pines
Wash drawing
approximately 6" x 7"

Forster's Tern
Sterna forsteri
North America
Wash drawing
approximately 7" x 5"

and so on. The range was about through five or six tones, and no two seemed ever to follow less than two full tones apart. The high ones seemed, when heard well and near, to have a slight tremolo. It seemed like some Grimm's fairy-tale bird, never seen, but heard, and luring the child on and on, and the woods are of a character quite in keeping with the illusion, so that one expects to see a witch's hut any minute.

I was going through the woods early in the p.m., and the idea came into my head to try and imitate the note, as I could remember it. I had hardly done so, when a beautiful reply came "a touzen times louder," from nearly over head. It was easy to make it continue singing, and the whole set of notes came, and mixed in was some chuckling and twittering which sounded natural, and finally I saw the bird . . . and cold-blood-edly pulled on it . . . it turned out to be a fine male varied thrush, a bird about the size and general build of a robin, but deep slate blue on the back and chestnut on the under side, with a black ring around its breast.

. . . The blowing and snorting of the whales, the screaming, way out on the bay, of gulls and loons, and an occasional goose, and, near by, the licking of the little waves in the pebbles and hum of a big bee, with just a thin "ray" of the hermit's song way over across the bay in the spruces, make the part of the picture that you see with your ears. The other part goes beyond my vocabulary, which has gradually become dwindled down to Wow and Gee.

Monday, June 12, 5 P.M.
. . . Cole and I went out at about 7:30, after an early breakfast, and were in the canoe until 1:00 after sea birds. The first bird I shot was a pigeon guillemot, which was the only one we got. Marbled murrelets came along with a delegation of five, and we got seven violet-green cormorants, five of which were males. I saved the two finest for me and the Thayers, and gave Fisher and Ridgway the rest. We have made a full study, comparatively, of the fauna and flora of this place, and have pretty full collections of the interesting forms.

Yakutat Bay, June 20, 1899
Well, after I finished the last log, I went up into Sitka to the Russian church and heard the service. It was very interesting and the chanting really very good and the more wonderful from the fact that most of the choir and all the Congregation were Indians. One old buck stood near me (everybody has to stand up or kneel on the floor) and hummed the bass to all the involved changes for two hours, scarcely making a mistake.

June 21, 1899
This a.m. we stopped at an Indian temporary hunting camp. It was the most picturesque place I ever saw, also the most sublimely filthy. Huts made of spruce bark . . . canvas tents, and various makeshifts were the dwellings, curious and ingenuous [sic] dug-out canoes, 20 or 30 of them, lots of painted squaws, bucks and children and a big bunch of mangy Indian dogs and the shore in front covered with all stages and degrees of vilely putrid seals—insides and bodies. One family

Gulls
Several varieties, not all distinguishable
Worldwide
Pencil drawing
approximately 9" x 7"

was boiling fat or soup or something in a sealskin tied up into a kettle shaped bag, in the corner of a bark hut. The old squaw was painted black, with white ears and chin and white around her eyes. They all paint up to hunt seals, to save their complexions!!

Tuesday night, 27

We are back at smelly old Orca [a salmon cannery] getting our wheel fixed. . . . After dinner this evening, a lot of the young 'uns took the canoes and a father apiece and went out on the level bay to escape the salmon in the air. And I was a little grouchy and home hungry, so I got hold of an Indian, whose name you can say by hitting yourself in the pit of the stomach and breathing in at the same time (can you do it) and rented his little 30 pound dug out canoe and long pointed paddle. . . . I took an ocarina for old times sake, paddled out by the good ship "America," loading salmon—a fine big old full-rigger—and paddled close under her great stern and then let the boat drift down the rocky shore, under the blue shadow of a great, rugged, spruce clad mountain, its top still snow and ice-bound, and the hermit thrushes fluting their clear music out over the water. It didn't take long to forget the grump.

July 1, 1899

Kodiak is a queer, clean little Russian town, with an old Greek Church with a chime of 4 or 5 bells, and no business portion to be seen. The fields are veritable gardens and are the first we have seen to have turf in

them. A few spruces grow on the slopes and alders follow up the damp spring runs to quite a height. The pastures smelled good and homelike and the willows and other things were very welcome and among all the strange rich alpine flowers we found to clothe the hill sides we ran across one head of common white lawn clover, whose fragrance was a sure enough old friend. . . .

Back at Popoff I., July 18

Fernow is playing Lohengrin, and the baby Harriman is laughing and playing with a cloth ball and things are generally cozy and pleasant. Everybody seemed to "get through" about the same time, so that we had a sing after lunch.

When we were up at St. Lawrence I. . . . some of us went ashore in a ship's boat against a hard wind and had a good hunt. Dr. Merriam got after a couple of polar bears, which, when he was near them, took wing, and flew away—swans! and the laugh was onto him. We got some good birds there, too, but by far and away the most interesting place we have seen at all was our next stop, at Hall I. We got there at about 7, and having had dinner early, a lot of us went ashore at once. We had seen many sea birds around the island and found that the cliffs were densely populated with nine or ten species of sea birds: one of those wonderful sights that I had heard and read so much about. But all description failed utterly to make the impression that the thing warranted, as it is truly the most wonderful sight I've ever seen. Thousands and thousands of birds—tame to stupidity, seated on every little ledge

Water Pipit
Anthus spinoletta
North America, Europe
Wash drawing
approximately 5" x 7"

or projection—from the size of sandpipers up to a great white gull that spreads five feet—all the time coming and going, screaming, croaking, peeping, chuckling, with constant moving of countless heads— all where you can reach over the cliff and catch the birds from the top in your hands. A pair of snowy owls had a nest right near where we landed, and the male and young ones became government property before they knew it. I spent a long time, all my patience, and a good deal of hard brain work and energy trying to outwit an old owl—probably the female of this pair—but she was too foxy, and I couldn't get anywhere near her, however I'd try, even by crawling through the wet sphagnum moss on my stomach for a quarter of a mile—but no go—I think foxes had tried every trick I had thought of long ago, and the old bird was up to her game in every detail.

Seattle—Portland
Monday, July 31, 1899

. . . We spent Sunday here in Seattle and are fast moving out for Portland, where we expect to arrive about noon tomorrow.

The ship has been practically dismantled. All the "art galleries," libraries, music, games, etc., etc., taken down and packed, so that it looks really as if it were all over, even to the extent of having said goodbye to some of the party who stop at Seattle. But the H.[arriman] A.[rctic] E.[xpedition] (termed in full Ham and Eggs) has resolved itself into the Ham and Eggs Club, with Mr. H., president, [and plans are for the club] to meet in full as possible once a year in N.Y., as often as it wants to in 2s and 3s. anywhere.

United States Biological Survey
Expedition to Texas, 1901

Fuertes was a member of a small U.S. Biological Survey team which worked in Texas during the spring and summer of 1901. The other professional members were Vernon Bailey, chief field naturalist of the survey, and Harry C. Oberholser, an experienced zoologist. The group had as its first handyman a man named Kelly and, after he was injured, the versatile Surber.

The purpose of the survey was to collect the skins of mammals and birds and to make a precise record of the wildlife encountered. Fuertes kept his own formal record in a journal, pretty much from day to day. How careful he was is illustrated by the following incident. In 1968 an ornithologist wrote to me to say that on this trip Fuertes collected three bush-tit skins. These skins, said the writer, were in the possession of Cornell University, and there was some question about just when and where they had been collected. After searching through Fuertes' journal, I was able to reply that skin No. 576 was that of an adult male taken on May 8, 1901, near Alpine, Texas, that 629 was an immature female taken two weeks later in a ravine in the Chisos Mountains, and that 638, an adult female, was taken on June 24 near Neville Springs and, at the time she was shot, was carrying food in her mouth for her young.

Fuertes wrote about twenty letters to his family while on this journey and one to his friend and teacher, Abbott Thayer—"Uncle Abbott," as Fuertes called him. Most of the letters were, like those from the previous trip, written on writing pads, one or two on single sheets of notepaper, and two were inscribed on postcards.

San Antonio, Texas, April 13, 1901
My dear father and mother and others,
I got here this morning in good time after a beautiful trip. I presented my letter to Captain Best and was nicely received. I am going to write you a better letter in a day or two and really tell you things—so don't mind if this is short and undutiful. I have a lot of birds to skin and several all skinned, but tomorrow is to see me afield by 5:30 as it gets hot early and I shall be glad to be in the cool skinning by the time the sun gets high....

Good night—the mocking birds are just stopping and a dark woman is singing across a little valley.

Sunday
There is a young man who preaches to these people once a month and he was up last night and held meetin'. I went as it didn't seem that anyone else was, but quite a bunch came, mostly women with babies, who wished they were anywhere else. . . . I don't think I ever did enjoy a service or a sermon more—but different. After meetin' I came home and went to bed to dream of the sweet music of the ranchman's wife and the solid shot of the young prophet of the plains. They was "Baptises." As the minister shares my room with me, I naturally had some interest in seeing how heavy he was on Sunday seeking and got so far as to give him a lesson in taxidermy on the Sabbath. He demurred a few tenths of a second, then, hoping that *I* would not break the SABBATH for him (I assured him

Common Snipe
Capella gallinago
North America
approximately 2" x 4"

it was my customary mode of spending it and he was all pleased), he watched two [birds] through to the bitter end and the last one, having been shot two days, had a very bitter end....

Langtry, April 29, 1901

Dear Family,

It's a rainy afternoon—the first since I left home—and as I have my work done, up to a certain point, I'll begin in a letter which may be finished later.... I haven't told you anything about this country out here.... It is all either great hot, nearly barren high plains or cañons.... The cañons are the places to go into; [they] form, from their improved water conditions, the finest kind of refuge for all the things that would like the climate of the country if it weren't so dry. These bottoms are generally grassy between the rocks and have good sized trees, live oaks, willows, and some others, which the birds like, and the rocks give fine places for hawks, eagles, cañon and rock wrens and other things to nest in. A cardinal or cañon wren can certainly make the whole big cañon ring with its song and it seems wonderful to hear a great clanging whistle, like a boy through his fingers, running from high up right down the scale in clear, deliberate notes—and look up and see, near the top of a 200-foot cliff—perhaps 50 or more yards up the cañon—a bird the size of a chippy [chipping sparrow], climbing around like a nuthatch on the rock face—the author of the thing....

Langtry is quite an interesting place in some ways. It has a great and only character in the person of "Judge Roy Bean—Notary Public, Justice of the Peace—Law West of the Pecos" (his shingle). One of the about three houses in Langtry is the "Roy Bean Opera House, Town Hall, and Seat of Justice." Said Roy Bean was here when the county was new and settled many queer cases according to his lights and his needs. He found a dead man once with $40 and a revolver on him—held a court and found the corpse guilty of carrying concealed weapons, confiscated the revolver and fined him $40 for the offense. Another time he had a case where one Mexican had killed another in a fight. In the court he searched him and found $7. Not wanting exactly to hang the greaser, he thought a minute and then said, "I fine you 5 dollars. Go home. The other 2 are behind my bar and any time you are by my place come in and you can have a drink." He eats here at the "Cottage Hotel" and has his place of business over across the S.P. tracks and his sign is, significantly, a gray fox hung by the neck.

Alpine, Sunday May 5

... We went with Hunter the Section Master at whose house we stayed, on the hand car over to Shimula 3 miles, to get a Mexican named Torres to take us on his horses over to the celebrated Painted Caves.... But we failed to get him.... The next morning, May 3, Torres came over with his horses and we met him and started for Painted Caves at about ten. It was a splendid ride, about 8 miles, partly over the high plain, treeless, but covered more or less with yucca, cacti and grasses; then down a cobble "military" road,

Winter Wren
Troglodytes troglodytes
Holarctic
Wash drawing
approximately 4¼" x 6¼"

about 20° down into the Pecos Cañon, across a mile or two of sand bottom, full of birds and brush, with a river ford—then up the other side and out to the old bed of the S.P.R.R. on the Rio Grande. The caves are about a mile down. There are 4 of them; we went to the farthest one, which is the biggest and finest. The cliff is about 350 feet high and the cave is reached by climbing up about 150 feet of heavy rock, dirt and gravel drift, grown with thick thorny bush of many kinds. When you get into the mouth of it though, you are back ten thousand years. It is a cave with an opening 300 ft. wide and 100 ft. high and is rounded into a hole running back 200 ft. The bottom slopes up 2/3 of the way and is then quite level and deeply covered with soft dust, full of fox and cat tracks. . . . The thing that gives the places their greatest interest . . . is the evidence all about of long dead human occupancy. The walls at the back of the two big caves still show the crude painting of some past people (Indians probably) in red and yellow. Huge figures 15 or 20 feet high still show dimly from a little distance, tho' from close you can scarcely trace anything. In some places there seem to be hunting pictures, showing deer feeding and great grotesque Mexican looking bear-headed figures in profile following or holding snakes. . . . At the back of the big cave there was a rank growth of beautiful maiden hair ferns and a tri-leaved ivy, rich light, soft green, as they grow in a perpetual half light. They looked so bright and clean in contrast to the dust covered antiquity all about them that one felt that they were artificial and crude, until they were looked at and picked; then the wonder of the place was still more enhanced. . . .

Torres exclaimed in a voice big enough for an elephant, yet soft and natural, amplified 100 times by the shape of the place—"here is water," and we went there and found, 200 feet above the river, a clear cold spring, the finest water we had seen in Texas and we were certainly ready for it. It was in the very back of the cave, and as we sat down to eat the lunch we had brought we noticed for the first time the glory of the view out of the cave mouth. Quite dark in the very back, then opening and lightening to a half lighted frame, the cave cut out a splendid picture of the Mexican frontier, which we saw through a continually moving curtain of cliff swallows, thousands of which were building nests in the roof of the cave. . . .

We left at about 3 and were home by half past four and I got my stuff ready (had only to pack my gun and a few skins) and waited for the train which was due at 5:30. It came at ten and all was merry (that wasn't asleep). The sleeper was jammed, so I stayed in the day coach and rode till 5:30 yesterday a.m. (Saturday) going to sleep and dreaming for hours, and looking at my watch to see that the hands had only moved 13 minutes. Well, after my day's ride on horseback and my night on the train I arrived at Alpine feeling very much like a broken bicycle crate, but I stayed around from 5:30 to 7 watching the night change to day. We had had a superb night—full moon —and when the east began to pale the moon was about an hour high, right in the notch of a 2000-foot twin hill, to the west of here about 6 miles, so as the sun began to pink the tops of it, the moon began to get filmy and finally went out, just before it set in the burning glow of the rising sun. . . . As the day came,

Green Heron
Butorides virescens
North America, Northern South America
Pencil drawing
approximately 3" x 3"

the various peaks, mesas, hills, ridges and blocks that frame the distance on all sides, and which had been of the same gloomy blue black in the moonlight, began to take form and distance—assuming each its own value of reddish, purple, blue or faint cloud color, as its distance, and direction from the sun began to have its effect. The twilight is so short here that the changes worked almost with the rapidity of the day-break scene in the peasant village in the play....

It is now the middle of Sunday afternoon, with the window open and a few outdoor sounds floating through and the buzzing of flies; an old blind man, who sits all day in the front-hall, coughs occasionally, my watch ticks in its fine baritone, and the hotel baby frets while its mother works or reads novels—can't tell by the fret which. It is pretty hot and lonely out in the sun, but though there is little breeze it is cool in my room. It is an east room and quite pleasant, wooden partition walls and ceiling painted lavender, an advertisement card of the "Riverside Herefords" cattle in the looking glass and a lovely lady, who uses "J. & P. Coats" spool cotton, smiling through misty blue eyes, looks at me sideways wherever I happen to be. But I don't care if she don't, so we get on fine. A little table, a good bed, and a wash stand that chronically swings open complete my menage.... I was counting up my results to-day and find I have skinned 96 birds, comprising 60 species and have made about ten carefully painted studies and a few drawings.

Tornillo Creek, Texas, Sunday, May 27
Dear Mother,
I have spent the greater part of the 2 days after a big

black hawk—that lives in the big cañon two miles below here, in the Rio Grande . . . I am going to get him if it is in me, as he is a rare and splendid one, jet black all over but a white bar on his tail. He sails around in the wind screaming, with his wings shut, all except at the shoulders, so that he looks like a kite.

Tornillo Creek, Texas, May 29, ᵧ01
Well, I got the hawk, and had an adventure in the bargain by virtue of which I spent a delightful hour in an hole 400 feet up a 600 foot cliff . . . The bird [a zone-tailed hawk] is a Texas record, and one of the very few U.S. records, so that when I had at last shot him, after three straight days of hunting him, it would never have done to let the splendid thing rot just because he fell over a cliff down into the cañon. I don't think I was in any danger any of the time, for when I found myself unable to go any further because of a boulder that was lodged in the fissure above me, and also at least unwilling to go down, I got O. to go for a rope. Then I sat in my comfortable hole, sang to a superb echo for a while, watched lizards and ravens and got rested for an hour, and came out all right, and the bird had by that time earned his record. I painted him fresh that afternoon, and am mighty glad of it, for all his lovely plum bloom has gone: he is still splendid, but nearly dead black . . .

Chisos Mts., Texas, June 9, 1901
My dear family,
. . . There is a big flat-topped mountain about six miles back of our ridge, with a lot of splendid timber on it,

Greater Antillean Grackle
Quiscalas niger
West Indies
Wash drawing
approximately 7" x 9"

Henicorhina leucophrys

White-breasted Wood Wren
Henicorhina leucosticta
Central and Northern South America
Wash drawing
approximately 9" x 7"

and B. was very curious to explore it to see if it had any chipmunks in it—for it would nach'ely haf' to be a new form. So we got aboard our ships of the desert at about 10:30—a pretty late start, to go around the range of the big mountain. It is also one of the highest points in the range, going up about 8,000 feet, and a pretty stiff one to go up. We expected to get back for late supper, so only took a couple of biscuits with bacon and peach stew in them, and my little quart canteen of H_2O. After a long hot ride up and down stony hills and ridges, and a good part of the way leading the horses to save them, we got to the mouth of the gulch leading from the great basin of the mountain, which reared its forested sides up a good 5,500 feet above where we entered. We found a good little open place with grass, picketed our horses, ate our grub and started up. It was just 1:30 then, and soon after we had entered the great boulder-jammed forest B. stopped short on a fresh trail, which I could also plainly see, of a big bear and one or two little ones. So we shut up and went as still as possible to get a clip at her if we could. We continued the silent habit all the rest of the way, which, though adding to the great impressiveness of the mountain, grew very tiresome— especially as we got up into the thinner air where we got tired and stumbly quicker. It was a very steep climb; the first half was up a boulder-clogged wash or stream bed, with a good many stiff climbs to get up. It was as dry as a bone, except for a little stained pool in a rock bed at the very foot, and as the sun was cooking hot we soon got pretty dry as we left our canteen half full at the horse camp against our dry return. But at its hottest, when we were nearly up the stream

bed, it headed up rapidly and began to hail, thunder and rain. We went into a cave, rested on an old bear's bed, and pretty soon each found a nice little trickle that we could sit under—and we got a nice old clean drink just at the moment we wanted it most. After that we struck splendid spring pools all along, and every concave rock held a nice little drink whenever we wanted one. Pretty soon it began to clear again, and it was fine and cool, the hail having worked wonders, and we continued our silent climb, ever on the look-out for bear or deer. Bailey wants specimens very much, and the one he got the other day gave us plenty of delicious fresh venison for a week—which was a true godsend, after our supply of bum Texas bacon had been a week "all" [gone]. Well, to get back to the trail: we kep' a-gettin' upper and upper, into the junipers and pines, and even spruces—(the same noble Douglas spruce that comes in Alaska!) and finally, at 7,000 feet, left the bed and took to the hillsides and made for the "high grass"—through half a mile or more of 45° smooth grass slope, sprinkled with tall-stalked agaves here and there, and all sheltered under a lovely orchard-like growth of gnarled old live oaks and nut-pines, as still as a church on week-days. At the foot of the comb-ridge, which all these mountains have, B. and I parted to work both sides, and met again in the stunted growth on top—8,600 feet above sea level, the highest I have ever been on my own pins. After quietly enjoying the wonderful view we got, for a few minutes, B. looked at his watch, and to our complete dum-foundation it was 7:15!! and the sun was about to set. So, though we had left our coats below with the horses, and our clothes were still a little damp

Snowy Owl
(Nyctia Nyctia)

Snowy Owl
Nyctea scandiaca
Holarctic
Wash drawing
approximately 9½" x 7"

from the soaking we had gotten (for we had decided to disregard the storm and push up and on) there was nothing for it but to camp, as it was a good three or four hours' climb down to the horses in the daytime, and probably six or eight very dangerous hours' work at night, and then we would have had to wait for the moon before the horses could start out, and it would be daylight before we got to camp. So we found a little cave under the comb-rock, and while B. rustled branches and grass for a bed I humped fire-wood, and by dark we had as nice a lair as ever bear or panther stretched out on. We built a little fire under a live oak log which we placed across the open side of our hole, and by moving up the sticks about once an hour (which I got so I could do without waking up) we kept our little cushion of air so warm that we both got a very refreshing night's rest, as we were both pretty weary. We tried hard to find a rabbit, pigeon, or something, but the biggest bird we could get was a chewink, and the biggest mammal nothing at all, though deer were all about us and we even heard one old buck stamp as he got up and out. But the brush was so thick that we couldn't see to shoot anything more than a rod or two away. So we went to bed hungry. We got up at daylight and separated to hunt again, with no better result, so, at 8 o'clock this a.m. we sucked the water out of the little dips in the rock near "camp" and started down. It took us until 11:30 to get to the horses, which were still there, plus a fine old hound dog which we "allowed" to follow us back to camp, where we arrived at about 2 this p.m. about as hungry and weary as they grow, I should say. We lapped up a few mouthfuls of food, to get in trim for

"chuck" tonight which is just now ready, so "YOU MUST EXCUSE ME, MAGGIE"—I eat.

biscuits——*bacon—*biscuits—*—*applesauce etc., repeat *ad lib*.

There, I feel better. We are truly lucky in our camp man, who replaces Kelly who broke his foot. He can cook to beat the band, and when the baking-powder gave out he quietly set to work and made up some sour dough, and we have those now, just as good as his b.p. ones.

We are still at the same camp we came to that first day—June 1—and will probably stay here for several days yet. We have got representatives of nearly all the birds, though there are two or three bully good ones that are yet to grace my little tray-full of Chisos birds. I have written my two hundred and seventh label, and while we have been here we have added about six species to the Texas list and two to the U.S.

Chisos Mts., June 18

Things began to happen there and I guess I'd better tell about them while things are fresh and go back to the mountain trips afterwards. Two men came to camp (owners of the range we were on) and had dinner with us and right after dinner we pulled out for this place, the "Dug Out." One mule was peculiar and refused, after his two weeks loafing on the range, to get into place and it took Surber half an hour to get him into the harness. We finally got off and by 5 p.m. got to this water, which tho' far inferior to the water we got at "Pine Cañon" does very well if we let it stand long enough to settle the alkaline mud it holds in sus-

pension. When grub time came it developed that our bag with nearly 60 lbs. of deer meat (our all) had dropped out behind on the trip. So cooking up all the bum bacon we had left and getting an early supper, Bailey started right out on Fiddlesticks, his wire haired steed, up the back trail for the sack. My horse Fannie had been turned loose to feed with one mule, Tobin. Fiddlesticks and Baylor, the other mule, were [usually] picketed, as the mules fall in love with the horses and stay by them and Fannie never showed any tendency to leave camp, where H_2O and corn are to be found.

So, with the extraction of Fiddlesticks, only Baylor, the mule, was left tied. We were all busy and didn't notice and while Fiddlesticks was away Fannie strayed and took Tobin with her, as Baylor merely wasn't enough to stay around camp for. Next a.m. Bailey took Fid. St. and went in early to the store to catch the out mail (a Mexican on mule-back) and I started out on one trail and Surber on another after the lost stock, which seldom strayed far from camp. You see we are all out of grub, nearly (B. found the meat tho' and got in at about 10:30 p.m. pretty well fagged, as also the horse) and wanted to take the wagon in to the store, 8 or 9 miles, for provisions. Our flour is "all," sugar, salt, bacon, coffee, oatmeal, likewise and we had on hand a cupful of lard, a lot of jerked venison, enough cornmeal, and there you are, all said. We haven't had any butter since we left Marathon, no condensed milk for two weeks (but we don't miss them) and no dried fruit for a good while either —that we do miss a lot.

Well, anyway, I walked 3½ miles back up the trail to the last fence and back, without a sign, and it was sure hot a whole lot, as they say here. Surber went 4 miles and back (our shoes are nothing either) over the hot stones and came back as sad as possible, reporting that the horses had struck the straight trail for Marathon (the nearest fence [in that direction] is 45 miles from here). We sat and got cool and hungry for about half an hour; then I took a list of the things we had to have and started on foot for the store to head off Bailey and get him to bring them in on Fid. St., and I would come back when I felt like it. So at 11 a.m., the beginning of the roasting, windless part of the desert day, I hit the shimmering trail with squinting eyes, and as few clothes as I thought etiquetty. I started out and got half way there when I met B., delivered my message and my responsibilities. He decided that the horses weren't very far off, [that] F.S. was too tired and hungry to go back to the store and [that] we could better go back to camp, saddle *BAYLOR*!!!! and catch the horses and then come in with the "hack" for the duffle.

That was so much easier than going on to the store that I was glad to have him take the responsibility and leave it so. So we took turns on the horse and got back to camp at about 1:30 or 2. We had a grub of venison and cold biscuits and then—now comes the climax of what has happened so far.

Surber was going to ride F.S. after the stock, but B. said he was too fagged: to saddle Baylor and he, Bailey, would ride him after the horses. Now Baylor is a big, strong mule that hates everyone in camp but Surber and he only stands him because he has to. Well, he took the saddle all right and Bailey got on all right

Ring-necked Pheasant
Phasianus colchicus
Asia
Pencil drawing
approximately 4½″ x 6½″

and started off, with Surber on a rope around Baylor's nose to snub him off if he got gay. But if a big strong mule gets gay, you can bet he'll sow more wild oats to the linear mile than any ten bucking horses that ever bumped. O. and I stood at camp, 30 feet away, and first off all was well and it seemed that the horses were almost caught; when all at once old Baylor's eyes sparkled black, his ears lay back, he got a good grip on the bit with his grinders and lit out like the Black Diamond Express, with little Bailey on his back like a boy. He tore loose from Surber in a second and went straight for a little gulch about 50 yards ahead, jumped it, landed on the other side with bunched feet and began to buck as only a big strong mule can buck. Bailey gripped his saddle horn, cut loose all other holds, and devoted himself to hanging on for dear life, and that is—seriously—just what it was. He succeeded for about 30 yards of liver-tearing, wrenching, pitching, bucking, when I saw the old mule give a great leap forward, and throw the little man head first over the crest of a little rise that lay between me and him. He gave a little yell as he left the saddle and I could hear the thud as he hit ground.

In almost no time, and with no sense whatever of the ground between, I was over there and O. was close behind and with the mule dashing head up through the brush ahead there lay little Bailey, on his face, having hit on the back of his head, rolled thro' a somersault and rolled over through the force of his terrific pitch. He was insensible and bleeding from somewhere on his head, or neck, or ear . . .

But when I called him he came to enough to say, "It's all right boys," in a dull way, slowly. And we

carried him back to camp and put him on his bed. When he saw the blood on my shirt he asked wondering if I'd been bucked off a mule or something. Well, to relieve you, as we were relieved, he is all right but for a headache, and a lame hip and shoulder, as he fell on a level place, covered over with small loose stones. . . . He came slowly to, and with the aid of some of the "critter" I brought with me, he was soon able to recall things up to the point when he got on the mule and he has never remembered what came after that at all.

So he sent Surber on poor old Fiddlesticks after the two strayed nags. He set out at 2:30 yesterday and hit the trail; came back about 9:30 this a.m.: no horses. Then thinking that they might be up over the gulch a way, went on foot over my trail of yesterday—no horses. Now he is getting grub and will start out again afterwards for another hunt. . . .

Well that about brings us up to the time being . . . I have to-day written up my notes for the two weeks in the Chisos mts. which makes me quite pleased as they are wonderful from a birdy standpoint and I was too busy while there to write a word. I have two kinds of birds from there new to the U.S., and several known heretofore only in S. Arizona, and a whole lot of mighty interesting stuff, as well as an idea of what desert mountains can be if "properly approached."

[*L.A.F. to Abbott Thayer*]

July [24?], 1901

It seems a year since you all showed us the last we saw of you in Berkshire last November—and I'm sure I

Sandhill Crane
Grus canadensis
North America
Pencil drawing
approximately 9" x 7"

Whimbrel
Numenius phaeopus
Holarctic
Pencil drawing
approximately 8" x 6"

hate the long apartness, and the way I have let being busy and scattered cut off my natural desire to tell you about the things and places that I've so much wanted you to see and enjoy with me. I've tried, in my letters home, to keep as much as possible of what has come my way before the home-folks' imagination, and I hope (though I didn't tell them to, I'm afraid) that they have sent you those letters as they did the Alaskan ones, as they have been written from time to time, mostly in the places they are about. . . .

The real thing that started me writing to you finally, is the trip up into the Sacramento Mts., in New Mexico, that I have just come down from. I was up there six days, and though I didn't find Mexican crossbills, which I had hoped for and expected, I did see, hear, and get a lot of other nice things.

The place is called Cloudcroft, and is 9000 feet up. The R.R. goes up from El Paso, and rises only a few hundred feet until it reaches the foot of the range, which is a great escarpment 4,500 feet above the plain. Then it goes back into a gulch or cañon and by winding back on itself . . . and turning 30° curves on a grade of from 4 to 10 percent, it climbs up through fertile valleys and gulches, higher and higher, into trees, orchards, farms, brushy hillsides, woods, pine forests, then mixing with junipers, till finally it brings you into the most superb primitive forests of immense yellow pine, spruce and balsam. It was like Alaska, truly, and some of the spruces (the same Douglas spruce, too) were 8 feet through, and probably 200 feet high. The ridges were all heavily forested, and between them were beautiful open glades with rich rank grass and profusely flowering pasture weeds,

and on the edge of these clearings, sharply different from the solemn darkness of the spruces, were groves of birch-like aspen trees, in which I fancied, going by, were all kinds of new Canadian birds. I got up there at about 7, got a box tent, and then went to supper. (There is a big cottage and tent establishment there, full of rather cheap people, but you can always dodge them.) When I came out, my whole sense outfit was set tingling with unexpected old-new sounds, for deep in the serene darkness of the spruces Audubon's hermit [thrush] was singing his marvelous song, and robins, Uncle Abbott, were caroling up in the tops. Then soon I saw a fine old red-fronted home robin running along the path, and I was so full of happiness at being in such a lovely place, and with these almost familiar sounds coming from it, that I longed for you to be there to hear it too. That made me think, though, that you were really hearing almost the same sounds and smelling the rich damp odors of the mountain woods yourself. The next morning I went out at sunrise, and it was cold and wet and delicately fragrant, and the woods were full of sounds—some I could place by analogy, like the red-shafted flicker, the slender-billed nuthatch, the red-backed junco, and the western house wren—and some were all new, and mysteries that had to be solved. I had a few splendid surprises, too, that made me gloat childishly. One of these was when after long debating as to whether I'd shoot one or not, I at last took a wing shot at a fine white-bellied swallow that kept flying over me and up to a big dead spruce-top where there were holes. He came twirling down, and I went up and saw before my popping eyes a superb velvety violet-green swal-

Hooded Merganser
Lophodytes cucullatus
North America
Wash drawing
approximately 5½" x 4⅜"

low! You can't imagine, from knowing a skin, what a marvelous beautiful thing this creature is when he is fresh, and his feathers stand out crisply from his body. The white is like the velvety white of a calla lily, and the head is a bronzy green, different from the rich soft blue-green of the back, and it is cut off from it by a delicate little collar of deep chinese purple which just marks the pretty little line of the neck. . . .

I've done more painting and drawing on this trip than ever before, and have really gotten together quite a lot of useful studies. While there is almost nothing in the way of bright or changing bill colors among these land birds, there is always a great charm and beauty about any well-shot fresh bird, and I've tried to make as many such pictures as possible, just because I like to, which is, after all, as good a reason as any.

It won't be more than ten days, probably, before I start home. I'm going to stop in Washington three or four days, then, straight home. I have thought the ground all over, and looking at things the way they seem really to be, have decided to do a set of pictures —thirty full figures and about sixty heads—of western birds I've seen, for Florence Merriam Bailey's book, *Handbook of Birds of Western North America,* to supplement Chapman's *Handbook of Eastern Birds.* . . . Home sensations and surroundings have so long

given place to those of railroad hotels and our "outfit," that it is only when I get a longed-for letter from my home or from yours that my senses are awakened to an understanding of the real greatness of that which they are getting along without.

My love to every one of you. . . . I don't really know which I want most—my own home or my Thayer home; in which ever one I am, I am thinking a lot about the other, and in each one I feel the same lovely feeling of being at home. And without any feeling of disloyalty to my real home, which nothing in the world but your lovely way of letting me be one of you when I am with you could bring about.

Uncle Abbott, you don't mind that incoherent spurt, do you? I know that often when I am in the midst of the splendid atmosphere of your-my house I don't seem to be awake to it—but I only need about three months away from it to show me how I miss it, and when it is eight months and bids fair to be ten—I am sure enough to warrant me in indulging in a little explosion of love for you all—which doesn't lessen in the least that which is stored up . . . by these years since I came to Scarboro' in the rain and began it all. . . .

There hasn't a day gone by since I've been in Texas that I haven't longed for you to hear or see some new or long-looked-forward-to bird.

American Museum of Natural History Expedition to Mexico, 1910

Soon after his return from Texas in 1901, Fuertes began a lifelong friendship with Dr. Frank M. Chapman of The American Museum of Natural History in New York. Chapman, a professional ornithologist of the highest ability, gave much of his time, during the period of his friendship with Fuertes, to designing habitat groups that showed bird and mammal specimens in their natural settings, with native grass, bushes, or trees against a painted landscape appropriate to the area. Chapman collected birds and their nests and eggs and took along with him another collector or two and one or more artists who made paintings of the landscape and kept careful records of the coloring of the living bird and the setting in which it most commonly appeared. Chapman had a high opinion of Fuertes both as a field ornithologist who hunted and skinned birds and as a painter.

With Mrs. Chapman and J. Lewis Bonhote, an English ornithologist, and his wife, Chapman and Fuertes made a collecting and research trip to the Bahamas in 1902. After his return Fuertes drew on his experience to paint a large and striking picture of flamingoes, which the American Museum still owns.

Chapman, who had visited Mexico in 1897, had a vivid memory of Mount Orizaba, in Vera Cruz state, and he and Fuertes planned the trip to Mexico for the winter of 1909–1910. Chapman thought the location well suited to display in a relatively small area a wide variety of living things, from the tropical life of the forests on the lower slopes to the near arctic condition at the uppermost timber line. For the entrance to the Hall of North American Birds at the museum a Mount Orizaba habitat group would be excellent.

Shortly before he left for Mexico, Fuertes wrote to a friend, Courtenay Brandreth, and described what he and Chapman hoped to do on their journey: "On Feb. 18 we sail from N.Y. for Progreso, Yucatán, go into the interior to Chichen-Itza, the famous and gorgeous old Mayan ruins, where that marvelous ocellated turkey lives, among other things of interest, then back to the coast and over to Vera Cruz by steamer, and in to Córdoba, a small town at the base of the great 18,000 foot volcano of Orizaba. Here we make a base, and run surveys (biological) at different altitudes, for Orizaba begins in the dry tropical, and ascends, furnishing its own refrigerating plant, through wet temperate up to perpetual arctic. Some interest attaches to that proposition. Then, leaving O., we head for Mexico City and then up the coast to Tampico, where we do our main work: a careful and zealous lot of study and collecting on and around the great lagoon running from Tampico a hundred miles or so down to Tuxpan. Here are spoonbills in swarms, ibis, herons of all sorts and conditions, jaçanas, rails and gallinules of many kinds, jays of sorts, jacamars—all the typically 'tierra caliente' birds. We'll be gone till nearly the first of May."

Fuertes wrote these letters to his wife, the former Margaret Sumner, whom he had married in June, 1904. At the time of the Mexico journey they had two children, Louis Sumner, later nicknamed Shub, born in 1905, and Mary, born in 1908.

George Shiras and Chapman Grant (the grandson of Ulysses S. Grant) were zoologists who served with the expedition; E. W. Nelson and E. A. Goldman were ornithologists preparing a definitive work on

Possible Mallard and Pintail hybrid
Anas platyrhyncos and Anas acuta
Holarctic
Pencil drawing
approximately 5½" x 7½"

---

the birds of Mexico. Ostos had been a Cornell friend
of Fuertes—hence, the reference to Spring Day, an
annual carnival-type college holiday.

The oriole mentioned on p. 51, Icterus Fuertesi, was
a new species and was named after Fuertes.

Mérida, Yucatán, March [2?], 1910
I have been in a strange world. We got here last Tuesday and went by sail through mile on mile of henequin (yucca-hemp) plantations, to Citas, and there Mr. Thompson met us with three *volans*—three mules per *volan* and over eighteen miles we bumped, tossed, lurched, and pitched at breakneck (literally) pace, and landed at Chichen—which I must tell you about later. Most wonderful ruins—so impressive that I all but forgot that the woods were ringing with cries and screams of parrots, motmots, and all sorts of new tropical birds. I stayed there four days, but the others only two, visiting other ruins. I collected about fifty birds, but lost out on the turkey, though I had about six Indians on the trail for all the time. We've seen Maya dances, social and ceremonial, and all sorts of strange and weird things. The Mayas are the most perfect people you ever saw: good-looking, strong, but above all gracious, courteous, simple, and honest!...

Here it's tropics, rain one minute in torrents, sunshine the next, but always hot daytimes, and cool and lovely at night. The whole surroundings and atmosphere are very Spanish—I can get along pretty well with it....

A few ticks got in their licks; but most over now—no bad suffering.

Just landing Friday p.m. at Vera Cruz. A bully trip from Progreso; Orizaba was in plain sight thirty miles at sea, ninety miles away!

Córdoba, Mar. 6, 1910
Your letter which came today was the chief event, so far, of the trip. You can't overjudge what your letters are to me when I'm so far away: I don't worry about you, exactly, for I know that you are where you can get advice and help if anything should go wrong, which it isn't very apt to. But when I've had a letter saying you're all O.K. at home, I feel as if I had a new start, and everything is right and I don't get blue when I get tired out, which happens every day....

You can't imagine what a sublime mountain old Orizaba is. It is only visible till about 11 a.m., when the haze and clouds always conceal the cone. But between 6 a.m. and 10 it is a great distant opal—pink-lavender with a moon-cold snow-cap extending far down the north side, its feet in velvet forest, and a foreground of tropical forest and light green sugar fields, with lovely warm old red-tiled white-walled Córdoba with its stately ancient cathedral (and *such* bells) I could hardly get my breath when I first went out, yesterday morning, to see it.

Córdoba, Mexico, Mar. 9
... The painting is exceedingly interesting, and every day the same thing happens to the mountain. At sunrise, it is crystal clear, and though it is about thirty or thirty-five miles away, every detail can be seen, with a

White-throated Quail Dove
Creotrygon frenata
Central America
Wash drawing
approximately 5" x 7"

glass, and it is a lovely pearly pink cone, white-crowned, rising majestically up and up into a wonderful clear blue sky. Its whole upper cone is bare of trees, and is very full of opalescent color, but the tree-line is sharp, and makes it look pale blue or lavender, in a straight line. Then come the still blue, but darker, foothills, very sharp and abrupt, forest-clad from top to bottom, and then the flat plain—like Africa, with open parks and pastures and occasional flat-topped trees, with a nice varied foreground. My kit is very compact and light, and easily portable. I've found a comfortable root under a big tree high above the road—made for me—with a most incomparable arrangement of picture.

. . . The other day [Chapman, Grant, and I] took a narrow gauge train up to Coscomatepec, 80+ miles up towards and around Orizaba, to see a view Nelson said was fine, and on enquiry (at 7 a.m.) found it cost more than we had to go up and back first class. So we went second, swarming with Mexicans and Indians into a sort of combination freight and cattle car and rode for 3½ hours. Arriving we were told that the train returned at "doce y media" (12:30) which sounds almost exactly like "dos y media" which is 2:30. So we were all hunting merrily in different places, and foregathered about 1:30 at the station, to find the train had gone back and none other till next day. So we counted up and found that above our railroad fare we had all told just $4.10 Mex with which to get 3 men 3 meals and a night's lodging. So we went a mile up to the ancient old town (where the weekly market was being held) and after looking around some found the village "guest house," which I'll later describe, and

found we could get a lodging for $.50 each, supper for $.50 each and breakfast (cocoa and bread) for 15¢, leaving us 15¢ etc. for individual expenses. So we hopped it and found a big, clean, tiled room with 3 beds (boards with a thin mattress and one blanket) and after a bully dinner of rice, chicken, soup, salad and meat, with hot black beans as dessert (a universal custom in Mexico) we went to bed at 6:30, cold and tired to a limp state, and actually slept 12 hours on those boards, getting up at 6:30. It was clean and nice; and a lovely old white haired Indian woman was our caterer, and did well by us and was grateful for the 5 cts. (Mex = 2¼ cts.) left over from the 45 cts. our breakfast actually cost (leaving us 10 cts. to face the world with). We hunted and photographed all a.m. and turned up from different directions at the station at about 11:45 and *caught* the train home. But it was a good experience that we all enjoyed.

St. Pat's Day, Mar. 17, 1910
. . . We all expect to embark on the hurricane decks of mules (Chapman, Grant, myself and a friend, picked up here, by the name of Patterson) to Orizaba's top-knot.

We've had eight days of either rain or dull weather, during which the mountain has been visible just thirty-eight minutes all told. I beat it out, one and a half miles, to where I've been painting, and had ten minutes in which I could correct my picture before the clouds shut it out. Some luck, as it was enough. It was between seven and eight a.m. I am in bully shape, physically, and have nothing worse than a number of

Skunk
Mephitis mephitis
North America
Black-and-white wash
approximately 9" x 7"

Gyrfalcon
Falco rusticolus
Holarctic
Pencil drawing
approximately 9" x 6"

large and small bites of sorts, and the nettle stings. These tropical nettles beat anything I ever heard of: if they get you when you're hot there seems to be no limit to what they do to you. I got stung the first day or so of my stay here, and though I've nearly nailed them by killing the skin with formaldehyde, they are still doing business. It's lucky I didn't get a bad dose for it would have done me up so far as doing any work is concerned.

Córdoba, Mexico, Mar. 21, 1910

. . . We have been making the best of the bad weather by side trips to various points along the down-end of the line. Motzorongo twice, where a regular hot-house condition of life exists; perfectly gigantic forests of silk-cotton and wild fig, with curious small palms and tremendous ferns, climbing vines like a ship's rigging everywhere, from wire size to the thickness of your body—reeking, steaming, moist, and where live trogons, toucans, parrots, all sorts of tanagers and hummers, queer new and unimagined birds, jaguars and even monkeys, and orchids of all sorts and colors, air plants unnameable, odorous of queer flowers and reeking with strange and very impressive smells, silent except for unguessable bird-notes. If it weren't for an old trail that follows the stream, it would be impenetrable: as it is it is a perfectly ideal collecting ground (except for the sweltering dampness and the mosquitoes) and more than anything else like a limitless hothouse of wildly strange exotic plants. Trees start out of the ground, and you come face to face with them so big that you have to stop and

plan your way around them. I shot four times at a little falcon from the base of one, and never touched it with my shot—or if I did, it was so spent that it didn't hurt him. I also saw, out over the open valley, a pair of hawks among the rarest in the world. No mistaking them, for they were as big as a redtail, and absolutely gleaming snow-white!! Fourteen years ago Chapman saw one in this very place, and if he hadn't told me of it I'd have thought I was dreaming. They looked wonderful and beautiful circling in the thin air against the great foliage-banked mountain side, and I watched them with my glass a long time. How I wish you could be enjoying some of these wonderful days with me. When I left I had no idea of the marvel of true tropics; and yet I've hardly seen a taste of it, for Córdoba is so high as to be strongly tinged with upland vegetation and birds—also so much cut out and so long inhabited that it is more like a farm country, only the *barrancas* being truly tropical.

Córdoba, Mexico, Mar. 28, 1910

We got so sick of lounging around the hotel or collecting locally in the rain, and time went on so, that finally last Tuesday (Mar. 22) we packed our outfit, Chapman, Patterson and I, and took the 7 a.m. train in an overcast and threatening day for Coscomatepec, and got there at 10, being on time. There, after some slight palaver, we got our two men and seven horses, two of which were pack animals, and after a lunch at the village tavern we started, about noon, on our twenty-one mile ride up to snow. It was still cloudy, and before we'd been out an hour it rained. Well, we went

Chuck-Will's-Widow
Caprimulgus carolinensis
Western North America
Wash drawing
approximately 2½" x 1¾"

on, and at about 5 p.m. came to a camping place on the 7,000 foot level. Here we made camp, and Patterson got our first meal, with wet wood—in an Indian's back yard. We were objects of keen interest, not to say open amusement, to all the Indians—the youngsters could not control their smiles, the men stood quietly around till dark, and every woman in the *iacal* was peeking over or between something. However, we had a good camp and a good meal, and broke at 6 next a.m. and pushed up out of the corn belt up into the zone of pines. The trail, by the way, runs the entire distance along the top of a knife-like ridge, or hogback, twenty-one miles long, with deep *barrancas* on each side; so that as we were in the clouds all the time, and could frequently look from our horses down into eternity on both sides, the sensation was much as I should suppose ballooning would be. Well, anyway, we went till about 1 p.m. and then found at 9,500 feet a perfectly ideal place, in the superb forest of long leaf pine and oak. Here, under an oak 120 feet high (guessed at) and ten feet around, shoulder high, we made our camp. In the afternoon we hunted, and I got a magnificent crested jay, of the Stellar's type, the gorgeous little red warbler—cardinal red with square silky white cheek patches—and a lot of other things. It was still in the clouds, and I shall never forget the beauty of the noble pines, as they faded into the mist or became distinct as the clouds rose through the *barrancas*. We collected again at camp till about six, when it gets suddenly dark, and also cold. After supper, when we were all sitting around our fire, Frank looked around, let out a yell, and there gleaming between the pines in full moonlight, was the glorious crown of Orizaba,

visible for the first time in two weeks!

I can't describe the wonder of it to you. It is the most marvelous thing of beauty I've ever seen, and when, next morning (after gazing at it for an hour or more and photographing it by moonlight) we got up in the dark and went out into the deep frost-silvered forest and watched it come into being, get distinct, and finally, while the deep valley was still black in shadow, catch the first gleaming ray of the sun, and finally get creamy, then rosy pink in a bluebird's-egg sky, our senses kind of left us, and we could understand why the Mexicans worship their snow mountains. From that moment, the peak was never long out of sight, though occasionally in the afternoon the clouds would drift up and hide it at times for a few minutes. Of the thousand varying appearances—never, indeed, twice alike—that were given us while we were there I can't tell you. It was my most marvelous mountain experience, and I shall never, I hope, forget any of it.

Well, after a glorious morning of admiring and photographing we broke this camp with a feeling we'd like to live there, and went higher. Passing through about 1,000 feet of cleared land, we at last entered the upper zones of trees (short-leaved pines) and got up to the high level of 12,000 for our camp. This was too high, for at night, when the sun set, the thermometer dropped in fifteen minutes from 57° to 12°, and we suffered (and the horses 'most died) from cold. Before noon the next day, the mercury in the sun was 112. 100 degrees' change in twelve hours! I think that's a record, and incidentally a hard thing to cope with. But we were all right, and in the morning we took the riding horses, and went up to the head of the

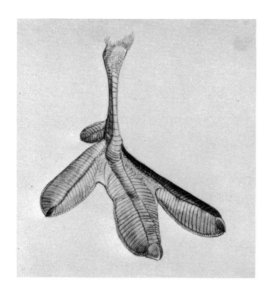

Foot of Horned Grebe
Podiceps auritus
Holarctic
Pencil drawing
approximately 5½" x 4½"

trail, at an even 13,000 feet. Here, I forgot to say, the Indians come all the way from Coscomatepec to cut ice, which they carry down in big squares, on burros and on their backs, to sell in the cities. Think of the strength and hardihood of these nearly naked Indians, to do this at this altitude. We couldn't climb thirty feet of hill without losing our breath and having our heart make a noise like a dog barking. . . .

To-day, when we got off the train here at Córdoba, the first thing we heard was, "Nieve" (snow), and when we'd cleaned up, and went out on the street to the P.O., it was ten minutes early so we sat down, and for the first time in Mexico, ordered ices on the sidewalk before the hotel. When we asked the boy where the ice came from, he said, "El pico, senor, del volcán" —the peak of the volcano! So we saw the whole thing, from start to finish. One of the most picturesque industries, I think, in the world, and very old and very romantic. . . .

Love to all, and I'm looking ahead for your long letters at Tampico.

Your Louis

Mar. 29, 1910

The trip up to the table land was very interesting and at times thrillingly beautiful. But our wonderful Orizaba trip rather tamed this jaunt to almost nothing. . . . All the whole landscape from Bocadel Monte to the city of Mexico is devoted to pulque cultivation— the booze they make from the immense century plants. All the day long, as far as the eye can see, nothing but pulque, pulque, pulque; it is tiresome and gets on your nerves to see millions of acres of good land exclusively given up to the making of the country's greatest curse. . . . It is really scandalous . . . and at the little stations the Indian women rush up to the trains with jugs of it —nasty sour—milk and cider smelling stuff—that looks like dishwater—to sell for one centavo a gulp.

. . . Coming up we passed a volcanic cone (13,000 ft. high, so with no snow) which is interesting to us nevertheless because about 3 years ago Nelson and Goldman were on it and G. ascended it to get the top zones, etc. He didn't come back when he'd planned, so Nelson, knowing the Indians jealously guarded the mt. as theirs and resented anything like prospecting, went up to find him. He found him in a hole in the ground, under guard, where he'd been kept for 2 days, and N. "persuaded" the Indians to subside, which they did. N. tells it merely as a joke on Goldman, but it was anything but that and N. doesn't seem to consider that he did anything out of the ordinary by going up alone to see what had become of G.

Well, dear, I'm going to bed. This is just thrown in and doesn't mean anything but that I'm thinking about you and sonny and sister and feel like talking to you before I turn in. . . . A week's freedom from ticks, fleas and bed-bugs has made me feel like a fighting rooster and I hate to think what Tampico will do to us. . . .

Louis

April 3, 1910
70 miles up the [Tamesí] River, Vera Cruz, Mexico
After a wonderful but rather tiresome ride of 24 hours we got to Tampico at 11 p.m. April 1, to find our mail

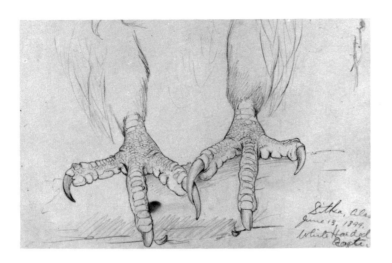

Talons of Bald Eagle (juvenile?)
Haliaeetus leucocephalus
North America
Pencil drawing
approximately 5" x 7"

(3 letters from you—hurray) and Shiras and Grant waiting for us. They hadn't been looking for us so soon though, and had planned to go up the [Tamesí] R. with a friend of Grant's, a Mr. Silsbee, who has a sugar and oil proposition up there.... Well, the invitation was extended to us and we thought it over and decided to hop it. So we got up at 4:30 next a.m. (yesterday) and had early breakfast, rearranged our outfit and took Mr. S. at his word, going aboard his launch, with our smallest outfit at 6:30 a.m. I can't describe that trip to you but it was wonderful. The first part of the trip—5 or 6 miles—is thru the lowland and there are big flats, where we saw 50 or 60 pink spoonbills, white herons, snakebirds, cormorants, many ducks and a million coots; and pretty soon great big mahogany and blue pigeons (the red billed) began to be numerous. The little kingfisher, as big as a sparrow and next minute one of the giant fellows— all deep chestnut below and as big again as ours—then a flock of squealing parrakeets and soon a pair and then two more of the big old regular, squalling yellow headed parrots. Rosewood trees, without leaves but a perfect mass of delicious pink and jasmine sweet blooms, show here and there among the dark green of the shore forest and made us crazy with their beauty. Great festoons of yellow jasmine and purple Bougainvillea grow over the overhanging trees, and the day long trip was an everchanging marvel of tropical scenes. When, at sunset, we reached the ranch, it was the loveliest place you ever saw, and the air right around the house was shaking with the screeching of three kinds of Parrots, big pigeons and great grackles and little fish crows. This morning, after a bully night

in our camp out in the yard, Grant went hunting after Peccaries and C. and I went out for birds....

Well we went out and in 3 hours I was back with 3 kinds of parrots in my bag, a pair of enormous woodpeckers, like those I painted for Nelson, two new orioles, a little black falcon, a big forest hawk, a red-billed pigeon and others and I had the fun of seeing three coatis—(the big, long-tailed and long-nosed raccoon that Ostos had that Spring Day) chasing each other around the trees, big black squirrels and other beasts and birds. As Chapman said, before we were out of the yard, "Great God, man, I don't know what to shoot," as there were so many things all at hand at once. So I shot at a parrot, which I didn't get and everything flew away. But I settled the question.

The little girl here has a lovely pet deer, fully grown and as tame and gentle as a kitten, the prettiest thing I ever saw. It is too tame though and you can't scare it away: last night it ate all the tags and licked all the pasters off our baggage and had the strings of my collar box all eaten before I noticed it....

After this jaunt and the lagoon trip, me for the choo-choos and the long back trail.

Your loving
Louis

Tampico, Mexico, April 9, 1910
Our trip up river... was wonderful, and each day brought new wonders. Three pairs of parrots, some parrakeets (four species in all), big wild pigeons, great red-capped woodpeckers like pileated all had nests right in the yard, and up the trail a way was an

Golden Eagle
Aquila chrysaetos
Holarctic
Pencil drawing
approximately 7" x 9"

immense fig tree fruiting, where there were always at least fifty, and sometimes a hundred and fifty or more parrots feeding. They are almost impossible to see in the trees, and the excitement of looking for them, without seeing one, and then having the tree suddenly explode into a screaming swarm of red and green birds is great. There were also great numbers of red-billed pigeons feeding there. The parrots are of two kinds, the big "yellow-head," the common big cage parrot that talks and whistles—all green with a yellow head and red in the wings—and one a size smaller, with the same body and wing coloring, but a red crown, and blue streak on the side of the head. The parrakeets are (two species) all green, with almost no color variation. There are big sloughs on both sides of the river where water birds—(snakebirds, white herons of all kinds, cormorants, etc.) were common, but inaccessible, as the lakes were full up of a kind of acacia, with pink spicy flowers and devilish hooks. Ticks were pretty bad in spite of swims in the river and cooperative hunts, we got pretty well chewed up . . . We were a week at the ranch, and I put up about ten birds a day.

. . . I found a parrot's nest, which F. took and is going to make a small group of for the museum. I also thought I'd discovered a new bird, a tiny oriole, but [it proved] to be only the tropical form of orchard oriole . . . a good bird nevertheless. . . .

Your Louis

Pájaro I., Tamiahua Lagoon
Mexico, April 17, 1910
This is the real thing. We left Tampico a week ago with a launch and two small boats, loaded with gaso-line and food and camp stuff, and the first night camped on the little canal that leads from Tampico into this big lake. I shot a lot of ducks (a pot-shot) and we had a good enough camp, though mosquitoes were very bad. Next a.m. we got a fairly early start, and expected to make Toro I., the first bird island, by 3 p.m., but as it got on toward 5, and the wind got up, and we weren't there yet, we decided to camp on the shore (east) and go over in the a.m. . . . So we all came in, and just inside the fringe of mangroves near shore was a rookery of about 200 pairs of spoonbills, with big young, with a few big white egrets, a thousand Louisiana herons, a few reddish egrets mixed in. . . .

There's no water on this island and we have to go to-day for more to the east shore, where we know a good well. I am again up against the proposition of having a wealth of elegant stuff at hand, so I go off whenever I can and do a little collecting on my own.

I got tired of spoonbills on every side and above and below me, so day before yesterday, I went out to the end of a long sand point at the far end of the island where the spoonbills go in ones and twos to feed (among cormorants, pelicans, skimmers, coots, ducks, plover, stilts and ibis) and dug a little trench in the shell sand and lay down in it. I hadn't been there three minutes when—whish—whish—whish—and bing came a rosy old cock spoonbill and sat down in the shallow water. So I shot three—all I can use—and brought them home, all beauties, and I spent yesterday painting their heads and feet, and skinning them. They were all beauties and I'm glad to get the spoonbill proposition out of my system. . . .

Black-necked Stilts
Himantopus mexicanus
North America
Pencil drawing
approximately 9" x 7"

Fortunately ticks are few in this island. They are frightful on the mainland and, between them and mosquitoes and the heat, collecting is difficult—to put it mildly....

April 21

Just then things began to happen and I had to stop. The boys cleared up the big island next day [April 18] and on the 19th we cleaned up in Frijole, so yesterday it was burst upon us that we were through!!!!! So yesterday at 8:30 a.m. we broke camp, spent last night about halfway and came through to-day and here we are, by golly, with nothing to do but get our party together, our outfit repacked, the birds off and then, "Ho for the land of our birth."

There are still a lot of things I want to get, but I wouldn't stay another week if I saw them skinned and dry and packed for home. I'm done—it's over—glorious in its beginning and its end—but I can't keep *heimlust* away any longer and now that I've come to a natural ending place I can't stay enthusiastic about anything but home. We're back before we'd thought we'd be, happy ... mournful, well—everything....

[Chapman's] getting a haircut while I have had a real bath, picked off (I hope) my last Tamiatura tick, and, overcome by the double shock, lie at ease on a real bed in the hotel, writing to my wife, dear, and letting dull care, in the way of open trunks, green birdskins, flying time, etc. bang at the door for once....

This a.m. we passed a point (Guzmann) where a big flock of ducks were lying ... and in one belch of our guns F. and I landed 3 tree ducks, 2 Canvasbacks,

and a Willett. So tomorrow we get Ostos and another benefactor to our cause and have a swell dinner at the Society restaurant....

Friday P.M.

I had to knock off then as it got late and I was also a little sick, having a few degrees of fever, due to strenuous overexhaustion and subsequent bathing in a draught. But it passed with the night and today I've been O.K. and done a good day's work, having rewrapped and packed all our Tampico birds—a large bunch. The main point, however, is this. We leave here tomorrow at 3:40 p.m....

Ostos came to lunch with us, off the canvasback and so forth we got yesterday, but when we got there the waiter assured us that the cat had eaten them!!!!! (one for each duck). I said I didn't believe it. So he brought in the mangled remains to show me and t-t-t-t-' was all r-r-right, something had sure enough, chewed up 3 out of the 5. So he got 3 teal from the market and it was perhaps just as good.

Well, dear child of mine, I'm on my way home and 'most there when you read this. *How* I long to have the journey over with....

I've had a perfectly wonderful experience, *wallowing* in new sensations and it's been glorious, but I've been pretty glum and felt mighty selfish at nights when I'd have time to lie down and rest and think. It's been my hardest trip and I've felt I must help Frank all I could ... so now I'm tired and ready to drop it. My dear child ... wait till I come....

Louis

American Museum of Natural History Expedition to Colombia, 1911

On January 3, 1911, Frank Chapman wrote to Fuertes: "I have just heard from Richardson and he confirms all I have read about the Cauca region; its beauty, abundance of birds, variety, etc. etc. The fauna changes in a mile from dry to wet and in one place birds will be nesting, while in another it is winter. Not in all Mexico or Central America, he says, has he seen such forests as are on the West slope of the coast range, and the opinion of a man of 30 years' experience, of course, counts. The region over the first range (Cauca Valley) is healthful and accessible, and the people are obliging; in short, Richardson's letter, added to a lot of other information I have recently acquired, makes it impossible for me longer to resist the call of Colombia. Only one thing is needed to make me say 'I'll go'; that is to hear you add, 'I will too.'"

On January 4, Fuertes replied: "My dear Frank, I greatly—oh gosh, how greatly—hope I can go with you to Colombia."

Soon they were off on another journey to collect materials for a habitat group. William Richardson of the American Museum joined them in Colombia, as did Waldrow DeWitt Miller, an ornithologist on the staff of The American Museum of Natural History. Bruce Horsfall, one of the staff painters at the museum, worked on the habitat groups in New York.

All the letters Fuertes wrote during this expedition were addressed to Mrs. Fuertes. In a preliminary note written before sailing, Fuertes had warned her, "I shall be so blasted busy making opportunities count that I shall probably write nothing but disconnected bunches of dope."

Sunday A.M. (Mar. 17, 1911)
U.S. M L 5 Advance

At last we are drawing in toward the end of our first stage and if all goes as it has been, we'll be in port at Panama sometime tomorrow morning. . . .

Ship's company small, but very interesting, largely made up of people engaged in the canal zone, and not least interesting among them a big young government *embalmer!* going down on his honeymoon!! with quite a pretty and attractive young bride!!! and he has the loveliest curly hair, seven solid gold teeth and uses violet perfumery which does not entirely cloak the formaldehyde of his profession. *She* confided to me that a dear friend of theirs was coming down later to take care of the bodies when the *Maine* was raised out of Havana harbor. . . .

I guess you better tell Sum[ner] that if he is awfully good and careful, and will never take out any but the records he can reach with his *heels on the floor* he can play the Victor a little bit each day. But if he drops or breaks any or hurts the machine in any way he will have to stop altogether until he's bigger. He enjoyed it so much, it seems too bad to cut it out. Use your judgment, however. . . .

Love to all,
Louis

Steamer Quito, *Fri., March 22, 1911*
We're about 30 miles out of Buenaventura now and I may have a chance to get this off on the "soon" boat if I write now and have it ready for mailing. . . .

The Pacific has been like a mill pond by day and

Blue-crowned Motmot
Momotus momota
Central and South America
Wash drawing
approximately 9″ x 6″

Pigeon Guillemot
Cephus columba
Northeastern Pacific Ocean
Wash drawing
approximately 6½″ x 6″

like a distant view of Broadway by night, so full of phosphorescence. . . . All today it has rained, but now, as we near the rain center, it is clearing and lovely. Many whales were around this morning, and a huge school of high-leaping porpoises, not very near, and three immense flocks of unidentifiable birds, like ducks; a S. Am. flycatcher boarded us in the rain and later an "old fashioned" common Ithaca kingbird did likewise. Gulls and terns of unknown types fly or float by on chunks of driftwood and last night the Captain caught a petrel but let it go, not finding us. Sorry, for they are among the hardest of birds to get. Shearwaters follow the porpoise and occasionally a strange petrel or cormorant shows himself for a while.

In a few minutes we enter the harbor or river; then it will be probably too exciting and interesting. We are all anxious to get to work and into old clothes. . . .

The Southern Cross is now high in the sky and the North Star has gone entirely below the horizon. We are in lat 3½ N. of the Equator, and three miles off are forested shores where perhaps—probably—the foot of man—red or white or black—has never been.

March 23, 1911

Off, in a launch. 6:30 a.m. for Cali.
Richardson has over 1000 birds.
All well, the work begins,

Love to all,
Louis

Cali, Colombia, Mar. 28, 1911

We are here. And in an extremely record-breaking space of time: just two weeks from the day we left N.Y. The mail that came with us as far as Buenaventura will probably take a week more to get here. . . .

B. is a beautifully situated place as seen from the sea, ten miles up a mangrove-lined river, but once there, you see a filthy, wet, bug-infested, fever-ridden collection of shacks and 'dobes, which we were only too glad to get right out of. . . . We passed one night at Caldas, at about 2,500 feet, and left at noon next day with all our outfit. . . . We climbed up and on and up and on until about four p.m., when we reached El Carmén, a little village near the upper timber line, where we had lunch, and saw a fight, and a real professional cock-fight, as it was Sunday. Then we pushed on, and by dark reached the first settlement at the edge of the upper forest, "El Tigre," where we spent the night at the *hacienda*. Then we left early next a.m. after a comfortable night on a hardwood bench and nothing but a sweat-and-rain-soaked horseblanket for both mattress and cover, and my pants for a pillow. I could have drawn the grain of the entire bench without looking at it for you, I was so familiar with it by morning. . . . We had a look around in the morning, as the rain had stopped and we could see down the valley. We rode about two hours, into the noble high forest, and into the rain. . . .

I was pretty wet when we reached the summit, 6,500 feet, at San Antonio, so I thought I'd take a look at the forest. It was sodgey-sopping wet, rain pouring with a loud slush on the drooping forest. The path was a soup of dead leaves, mud, moss, etc., from three inches to knee deep. Every tree and vine was inches deep with spongey moss, wonderful flowers, deep blue, white, yellow and red, and ferns growing out of

A. A. Fuertes

American Bittern
Botaurus lentiginosus
North America
Pencil drawing
approximately 6" x 3"

every fork, and orchid plants in every bunch of moss. I spent an hour in this wonderful country, and shot some ten wondrous birds. I only had my pistol, so I couldn't get the big things, like trogons and toucans. We left San Antonio (which is only a road house, kept by an Indian woman, whose three-year-old girl was sitting in the door as we came up, *smoking a big black cigar*!!!) at about 2 o'clock, after our mules came up, and my clothes had dried a little. . . .

We got in late yesterday afternoon, in time for a good dinner: our first square meal that day, though Apolonia, the Indian woman at the ridge, roasted us each a plantain, and opened some sardines! The combination of dinner, bed the night before, and two days' riding were too much for me, and when I flopped down, right after dinner, on my half-inflated bed, I passed away immediately, and when C. woke me up at 10:30, I only lasted long enough to finish blowing up the bed and get back on it. I slept then solid till 6 this a.m., when I got up and skinned my yesterday's birds. R. has about a thousand birds here from the mountain region about San Antonio, and I have been much interested to look them over. . . . It is *marvelous* country up there; awfully wet, but cool, and *free from insects,* with an abundance of good water. . . .

A drink of Aguardiente costs some ten dollars; and it would have given you a jolt to see a little boy, driving a pack train, curve up to the bar at San Antonio— his legs barely reaching the sides of his horse and call for his Aguardiente, guzzle it, roll off ten dollars, swear at his mules and pass on: a *man,* at 6 or 7. . . .

I will write whenever I get a chance, and send the letters in, and they'll go out as soon as the people here

have decided they might as well go as lie around. You can put a brick on the table here and it will be there when you come back in fifteen years!

San Antonio, Mar. 31, 1911
This is the biggest stroke of luck you ever saw. We took any house we could get (there are only four in San Antonio, summer houses of Cali people) and it is a peach: lots of room, beds, chairs and tables, washing and cooking things *ad lib. . . .* I have put in the last two days in the forest, and have made up about twenty skins from this region. Our house is about three-fourths of a mile from the ridge, and near (though not in) the big forest. This afternoon I got a great black bird, as large as a crow, with a chestnut belly and a big orange ruff on the throat. Trogons and toucans are quite common, though not easy to get. The difficulty lies in finding what we have shot after it is down, as unless you mark it exactly as it falls there is no hope, the undergrowth is so thick, and there is so much trash on the ground: dead leaves as big as our dining table; moss, soft and soaking, a foot deep; and sticks and dead wood and leaf mold to any depth. Hummers are lost four to one found. I have done very well in quality, having landed some fine birds—some of which Richardson has only taken once, in sixteen weeks' work here, and I've only a small proportion of lost birds so far. . . .

We hunt the woods till about 10:15, when we turn back, reaching here about 10:45 or 11. At 11, we have our real breakfast, which is a corker: a great big plate *full* of soup, made of meat bones, rice, plantain, and

Herons and American Bittern
North America
Pencil drawing
approximately 3¾" x 5¾"

vegetables, all we can eat of beans, and such birds of the day's bag as are big enough. After breakfast, in dry clothes and well fed, we sit down at the long table on the east porch and skin our birds, which we can generally clean up by about 4:30 or 5. By that time dinner is ready, and is much the same kind of a meal as the 11 o'clock breakfast; a good solid square meal of soup, beans, and stew, with bully coffee. . . .

I'll knock off for now, and finish another time. Good night.

Sat. night

As there are reasons why one cannot spend his Saturday nights in the good old traditional way on this ridge, I take my pen in hand once more. There isn't much to say: I could describe scenery, or tell you how many and what kinds of birds I got, or how long my beard is, but statistics are dull. I went down the side of the mountain to-day, and got into a tangle that made me so mad I nearly cried. It is exhausting to the very limit, and when you are all soaked, and hot and sticky, and every one of ten million vines has hooks or brittle thorns that break off their points in you, and all conspire to baffle you in every tiny movement, it gets so wearisome that at times you want to yell, and hit back. If you do, however, you get all the skin scratched off your hands, and probably your face too. So just smile and be gentle—relax, in other words, and all they will do is take off your hat as you turn to look for a way out. Never mind, put it on again—off it comes again, then, while thinking what good control you have, *bing* out goes the root you were standing on

from under you, and you slide fifteen feet down a clay bank covered with climbing bamboo. Lest you think, however, that I am complaining, I will say that this place is free from all kinds of bothersome bugs, and the forests are gloriously rank and riotous . . . masses of scarlet flowers tip the ends of vines that fall from the treetops; queer human whistles mingle with whoops and hermit-thrush songs, and owl-like hoots, with the thrilling buzz of a gorgeous hummer as he shoots past, or hangs with waving tail too close to shoot at. That was just an incident, we get so tired at the end of the morning that little things seem big, and everything for the time goes wrong, or seems to. . . .

I got a hummer today that is the slickest little trick you ever saw. They are quite rare and I was lucky (and I may say skillful) in getting this one. The forest is too thick, and the deep tangle of trash on the ground so full of holes and so criss-crossed with climbing grasses, moss, sticks, dead leaves, flowers, and everything else that a small bird is almost invariably lost in it, even if carefully marked down. Miller killed a big oriole . . . this a.m.; it fell dead, straight from the tree, and he never found it, though it is black and chestnut, with a bright yellow tail and as big, actually, as a crow.

Here is a stopping place. It's 7:45 (late) and my candle will just last me to bed. Good night, please write.

Wednesday, April 5

I've let several days go by, as they are much alike, and we are so busy that it is awfully easy to go to bed after supper, and there's no such thing as writing at any

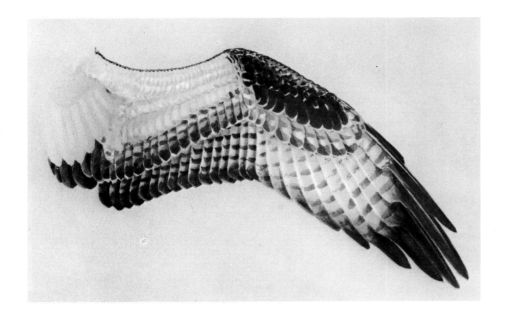

Wing of Osprey
Pandion haliaetus
Worldwide
Wash drawing
approximately 7" x 9"

other time, especially for me, as I have to do the best I can with collecting and skinning, to say nothing of painting every old bird that comes in with a blue face, green bill, or purple feet, besides detail of flowers, leaves, and the big drawings and paintings of the group. As that is what I'm here for, I feel that here, at least, I ought to hold myself ready to do anything that is suggested. I'm now about through with my part of the group work: I have painted and checked up the study for the background, and made notes of forest-colors for Horsfall to use and done a lot of flowers, etc., and have also, in the week we've been here, put up about fifty-five or sixty birds, including several doves and trogons, which are possessed of tissue-paper skins in which the feathers just stick by special favor of heaven. Yesterday I shot *and lost* a beautiful small trogon which I called for half an hour. Killed him dead, went right to the spot, hunted *over an hour,* and couldn't find him. Later I got a perfectly magnificent big trogon, as big as a big pigeon, with long bronzy-green feathers that fall over the tail and wings—and a beautiful nasal crest and a *rose red* eye! All his plumage above and on the breast the most gorgeous metallic emerald green, with gold and blue reflection in different lights, wings black, tail black with big white side feathers, and entire under parts blood-red. Next to the Guatemalan quetzal, he's the finest of all these birds.

To-day I went back, and *found* my lost trogon. A big spider had eaten part of his head, otherwise he was perfect. I also to-day got the best bird of the expedition so far; a big shy tinamou, or forest grouse, weighing about five pounds—a queer, elusive thing that may be new. F.M.C. has never seen anything like it. It is

ashy gray, beautifully pencilled with darker, and really belongs with the ostrich family. We had him for dinner tonight, and his meat was as white, and as sweet and tender as a partridge, and enough for four hungry tramps to get a square feed off of. . . .

Sunday noon

Strange as it seems to ao things on time here in Colombia, we actually got our horses up from Cali yesterday . . . by noon, had them packed by one, and started down the twelve mile trail for Cali, bag and baggage, by 3:30 p.m. It poured nearly every step of the way, and at times the trail was like a roaring river. From the ridge we could look a couple of thousand feet down into one valley where the sun was shining and the stream a tiny sighing thread of white, on the other side a deep purple shadow of thunder-clouds, long slanting ribbons of rain drenching everything, every gulley the bed of a roaring stream of clay-stained water, and a regular river at the bottom. . . .

This will reach you sometime—probably about the 24th, depending on the local authorities who consider the world outside of Cali as an entirely negligible quantity of no importance. We 4 are the only strangers in the city of some 25,000 people. It's a quaint place, everything handmade, without the use of any heavy machinery . . . actually unspoiled by traffic with the modern world. I'd like to get really into the life of it, just to see how it felt in the middle ages. . . .

Yours,
Louis

Black Terns
Chlidonias niger
Holarctic
Pencil drawing
approximately 7" x 9"

*"La Manuelita," which is the Eder sugar ranch
at Palmira, Colombia. Good Friday, 1911*

As per schedule, we left Cali last Monday at noon, and crossed the Cauca, river and valley, and landed on our feet at this lovely place at dark. But the best thing that has happened yet was that yesterday a mail came in, with your first letter, written just after I left New York....

To-day I went about a mile to some old forest, and heard the howler monkeys, big red fellows that bark like a lion—full as loud—and make a tremendous roar like the howling of a gale of wind through big trees. Macy [Eder's ranch superintendent], who had Frank's 22 rifle, shot a great big old roaring male; it is a little uncanny, as the beast is certainly a human-looking thing, with his hands and his black face and long dark red-brown beard.

As I am just stealing time to get this off to you to-day and have 14 birds waiting for me downstairs, I must stop now.... Love to you, dear, and to the kids and mother. Have all the fun you can get.

Louis

*"Miraflores," 6,000 ft. up on the
central cordillera, April 24, 1911*

We have been up here now for over a week, and though we are in a good house, with a family to look after us, and have therefore all that we need as to food, shelter, and general care, we are as thoroughly out of the world as I have ever been. Before I forget it, I want to tell you about "Rita," our cook. She came up the day after we got here, in the convoy of our "major

domo's" son, Francisco, on the deck of a black mule. As she loomed out of the valley, herself as black as night, with a long tightly-swathed black shawl, she was surely the real thing in spooks. Tall and slim, sixty plus years old, she wears for daily use, as a waist, a naively inadequate towel, so arranged as to be no good at all, either for purposes of warmth, concealment, or even mere decoration: when she can get one, she also wears a long black cigar between her bare gums, for she has no teeth that ever meet. Her lanky arms are welted and scarred so that they look like black-snakes run over by a train, and her wool is cropped short. She is simple, good-natured, and kind, thoughtfully feeding the whole family out of our stores, which have consequently to be replenished every few days....

The mountains are simply immense; the view of the Cauca valley at our very feet and the Western Range are ever changing and marvelous. In front of the house is a flower garden—great red hibiscus forms a 20 foot high border and within are chiefly roses and *sky blue* hydrangeas in clusters as big as a watermelon. Rare and beautiful hummingbirds are all day long buzzing about among them and overhead, every morning at exactly 6:10 a screaming flock of 27 yellow faced parrots (new to all of us) settles some 3 miles away at the head of a wonderful gorge in the Mts. I got one the first day ... since then none have been taken.... These forests are of immense—unlimited extent and there is no going anywhere but where the wood cutters have cut trails or the little water trails, cut along the mountain side to supply the little farms, offer a narrow path and clearings.... It is so dense, and the tangle is so complicated with nettles *(trees)*,

Cooper's Hawk
Accipiter cooperii
North America
Wash drawing
approximately 6½" x 5"

Left foot, Ivory-billed Woodpecker
Campephilus principalis
North America
Wash drawing
approximately 6½" x 4½"

thorny vines, needle palms and fallen trees, you may shoot a parrot, say, 50 feet away in a tree top and he'll fall 200 feet before hitting anything and then roll and flutter 200 more before stopping. When you go after him you discover that what you thought was ground is really a network of fallen trees, vines and tree tops, and solid ground may be 20 or 30 feet further down; a fat chance to find a wounded bird. So we have to figure carefully as to whether there is a chance of getting everything we shoot, so as not to waste life (and shells) to say nothing of time....

The birds here are fine—many kinds—probably at least twenty—of hummers, four of parrots, at least three of beautiful trogons, four of toucans, and any number of strange small birds, with queer noises and songs. Of course the insects are wonderful; all kinds of queer, enormous beetles, gigantic spiders and tarantulas, etc., etc., and butterflies beautiful beyond description. The forests are clothed in moss, out of clumps of which grow wonderful orchids, air plants of all kinds, and all hung together by a network of vines and "wood-ropes." Gorgeous green and scarlet trogons glide and swoop through them, and parrots yell up in the lighted tree-tops, but on the ground it is nearly dark, and queer little birds run around among the ground plants, never taking wing, but calling like rails, almost under foot but never visible. Some of the very most common have not yet once been seen, though the forest rings with their whistles, and we can at any time call up two or three to within a few feet of us. Curiously silent motmots glide up from near the ground and sit motionless in the vines, while way up in the distant tree-tops giant orioles, like the big

one I brought from Mexico, bark, scream, and hoot, up-side-down, and crackle their bills. Dark-colored forest hummers come and swing buzzing a few inches from your face, or light close by and look you over fearlessly. Way off down the mountain a forest quail rolls out his musical whistle, curiously distinct, "Cavalry kevelry cavalry," the first and last syllables of succeeding phrases overlapping, as if two were doing it. But I watched one the other day (and lost him for my pains) and it is a *one*-bird stunt....

Of dangerous animals and snakes we have seen nothing, and do not expect to. There are ocelots, and probably jaguars, somewhere in the mountains, but to get them requires special effort, dogs, guides, etc., which is not worth while. You needn't worry a minute about my being in dangerous country, as this is all as safe as West Hill or Newfield, and the people as friendly and a lot more interested, as strangers are about the rarest thing in these mountains, and I've no doubt that we have been the subjects of many an interested discussion. We are generally considered doctors, collecting birds for certain rare medicinal purposes: extract of hummingbird being a cure for rheumatism, etc., etc. That they can understand, while the entire idea of science or interest in the things we collect [is] beyond their comprehension. So we sit tight, let 'em think we'll sell the juice of the birds to cure men's ills for much fine gold, and thus retain their respect!

Wed., [April] 26
On one cup of coffee, and *nothing* else, I this day hunted the high mountain trails, about 7,000 feet, from

Green Herons
Butorides virescens
North America,
Northern South America
Pencil drawing
approximately 6½" x 3"

6:20 a.m. till 1:20 p.m. As our whole time and interest go into this bird business, there's little left to write about, as nothing else makes a dent. . . .

I went up, to-day, toward the top of this range, to a trail I discovered some days ago, where I've seen or heard some good things, and after shooting a green toucan out of a high tree, in thick fog, and spending over half an hour finding him (as you have first to cut your way through vines and nettles, etc., to where you think he fell, and then lay the place bare, or open it up so you can see the ground to hunt him, when half of the times, at least, he got caught in vines way up above where you can't possibly find him). Well, this time I found him, and he was a long way, by the watch, from where I stood when I shot him, though not more than thirty yards. But most of the thirty yards was up and down, and not much on the horizontal. Well, as I said, after getting the toucan, and losing some other things, I was at last in a very dark, deep, and damp part of the old forest, looking for a little brush-wood bird I'd shot, when I dully became aware of what I would call at home the noon whistle of some distant mill: a steady, very slowly rising note. Then I thought of a toad or frog and then again of an insect, like a locust. I timed it, three times, from the first I could sense the sound, as it began with nothing. The watch was 54, 57, 48 seconds, the longest consecutive note I ever heard any creature make. I imitated it, whistling inward part of the time, and the third time it answered, to my amazement, it was only a few feet away. . . . So I knew it must be a bird—for nothing else would come so quickly to a call, and I froze still as a stump. It was foggy—thick and dark

with clouds, and almost black in the densely shaded place I was hunting, and as I searched the gloom, trying to distinguish things, a ghostly shadow of nothing glided out into a small space more open than most, and there, only about 20 feet off, stood a big-eyed spectral bird; whether tinamou, thrush, quail or what, I couldn't tell, as I could only half see in the dark. But I've had my troubles looking too long at new birds before doing anything about it, so I instantly pulled up, in great and wobbling excitement, for here was a new bird, of wonderful interest. In my haste and excitement I did what I've often done before, and probably shall to the end of my days, and pulled the wrong trigger. Instead of a clean little pop of my "aux" BLAM went the other barrel, and a great hole was torn in the ground some 20 feet away. Hoping against hope that I'd almost missed, though feeling sure that I'd nailed him, I ran over, only to find that I had literally annihilated a splendid, rare—possibly new—bird. There was a mass of mud, meat, feathers, dead leaves, strung along for two yards. The main remnant, however, had the bill, part of a wing, a few feathers and one entire foot still held together; enough to see that it really was—or had been—a new species to us. As we'd never before heard this note, and as this family are all great and continuous callers, the chances were that we should never get another chance at it. You can be sure I was sick, and I sat there too chagrinned to even swear, looking at my poor bunch of had-been bird. Anyway, I resolved to keep that wonderful note fresh in my mind, to make a note of at camp, so, still sitting where I'd torn open the ground, I took out my watch and practised it "by the clock." I had done it

Rufous-tailed Ant Thrush
Chamaeza ruficanda turdina
South America
Wash drawing
approximately 6" x 5"

three times, when a sharp "wip-wip-wip-wip," right at hand, made me look sharp. This note I heard yesterday, up in the top forest on the ridge, and couldn't locate. So I "wip-wip'ed" cautiously, and kept still with my eyes open and gun ready. A few still, tense seconds, and this time I was ready and willing, and pulled the right barrel, and had the excitement of going over and picking up a beautifully shot and perfect peach of a little long-legged, big-eyed thrush-like bird, doubtless the mate of the male I had blown to pieces.

It sounds very cold-blooded, and I am not gloating over the killings so much as the virtual discovering, calling and identifying of a probably new species of one of the most difficult as well as the rarest tropical forest birds. Well, this is getting very long, and it is getting very late—8:30 in fact, and everybody else is in bed. So I must go too.

It's Friday night, and raining like the devil, and it has been since about noon.... When it rained the other day while we were in the woods, Roso (the native boy Richardson picked up) without a word, and quite as a matter of course, cut off and handed me a giant leaf —a lily—about five feet long and three wide, another for himself, and though it poured (as you know it can in these parts) we were as dry as could be while the shower lasted. Although there are tree ferns all through the forest here, at all altitudes, up at about 7,000 feet they get to be almost the predominant tree, touching each other, and forming a filmy curtain of lace about thirty feet above the ground, and making a most lovely sight. Of course there are giant trees of all species, too, that make an entirely independent

forest, way above, and all manner of vines, "wood-ropes," and creepers, hung deep with mosses, out of which spring beautiful ferns, drooping, like the finest "Boston" ferns, many feet. When it is clear in the woods, the mass of greenery, and the immensity of things, both in size and variety, is sort of stupefying, and you feel damned small and insignificant and wormlike, and have a strong tendency to whisper instead of talk out loud; but when it is foggy, all the infinitely complicated background is lost in gray, and you get the most beautiful silhouettes of enormous trees, isolated more or less from the great forest mass, and see the wonderful grace and form beauty of the host-tree and all its beautiful parasitic decoration. The whole stem of the tree becomes a great fernery, for a starter, and then wonderfully beautiful great tropical lilies send out gracefully curved stems with "elephant ear" leaves; pineapple-like plants grow in flowering masses from the joints of the limbs, perpendicular wood-ropes, trimmed with hanging gardens, come from the distant tree-tops, and root in the ground, and a little distance away the theme is repeated, with variations, one shade less green and one shade paler in the gray of the mist....

Cali, Colombia, May 10, 1911
The end of this week or the first of next comes the little stern-wheel steamer "El Sucre" which will take Frank and me to Cartago. It is two days to Cartago, as the boat ties up every night, and then eight to sixteen days over the Quindio pass in the main chain of the Andes to Honda.... I skinned my 360th bird this

American Coot
Fulica americana
North America, Northern South America
Wash drawing
approximately 5½" x 4"

afternoon. . . . If I get another hundred I shall think I am doing very well. . . .

I've been fortunate or otherwise in having been stung by this queer country's queerest bugs. One lays an egg in your skin and in a month or two a thing as big as a cashew nut has developed [which] transforms [itself] into a large fly and comes out. . . . Then, I've at last got chiggers—the toe-nail sprite toe nail chiggers. But don't worry: I can love them all and shall when they are big enough to reach. Love to all, and good night.

Louis

Later bulletin. Chiggers *out* and disposed of.

Latest bulletin. Steamer for Cartago now in port of Cali. Starts tomorrow, May 13; from now on the way is homeward. . . .

American Museum of Natural History Expedition to Colombia, 1913

Fuertes and Chapman's second journey to Colombia had its beginnings in the spring of 1912. On May 3, Fuertes wrote to Chapman saying that he had nothing to cause him to visit New York "except to see you, old party, and get a re-infusion of Orinocitis or Andesaemia, and so I'd better stay home." He added, "I've accomplished little since I came back last time [in the spring of 1911], tho' I've tried to stay on the job." He wrote again on September 17: "I might slip down for a few days. . . . I am so full of questions re . . . proposed S[outh] A[merican] plans." Already he was well along in the planning; "I am limbering up on a line of Biological Survey stuff. If all goes well we ought to be able to knock off about the first of the year and, as I shall need a good roast by then,—Santa Marta, good forr starta; so commencia, Villa vicencia; verra well suita, good place for shoota, etc. ad. lib."

In a letter to Dr. Isaac P. Roberts, another friend, on October 6 he spoke of an illness which left him with an irritation in his throat. "This I hope entirely to relieve by . . . going about January 15 to S[outh] A[merica] with Chapman"—where he could get his "good roast." On October 10 he said to Chapman "Am beginning to shine up my Castellano, likewise studying over my now identified collection [of Colombian birds taken on the previous trip]." Two days later he set forth a firmer statement of the plan in writing to still another friend: "I am trying to get my winter's work done by January 15 when I hope to join Chapman again and return to Colombia to carry on the exploration of the faunal areas of the Andean region in that country. It is a sort of center for distribution [of types of living things], leading as it does into the Ama-

zonian, Orinoco, Magdalena, Cauca, Patia (Pacific) drainage basins. Most interesting as viewed in the light of origin and distribution of types."

However, by November 12, Fuertes appeared to have abandoned the whole enterprise. He wrote to Chapman saying, "I now feel doubly virtuous in my decision to stay at home for it has come to a pass where I must be Quixotic or I become an ass." He left this letter unfinished and unsigned, perhaps on his desk. When he returned to it a little later, he added a penciled note: "Found this staring me in the face when I got back. Right there I changed my mind and began preparations to go."

He wrote to the Thayers on December 20, 1912, and by that time the whole journey and his part in it had come into clear focus, though, as on other journeys, the thought of leaving his family disturbed him. He said he was going "away with less of a feeling of sneakiness than I otherwise could; though as the time draws near I feel mighty mean about going. There is no way out, however, as my part of the expedition is the pivotal point and I must go. We intend to go up the Magdalena River in Colombia to Honda, then work slowly up the plateau to Bogotá, on east to the high paramo of Chingassu (14,000 ft.) and then down to Villa vicencia in the Orinoco drainage to only a few hundred feet elevation. Then back as we went in, and home about mid-May."

Besides Chapman his companions on the trip were George K. Cherrie, an experienced traveler and ornithologist on the staff of the American Museum, Paul Howes, who was also a painter, and two young amateurs—Tom Ring, who paid his way and who went

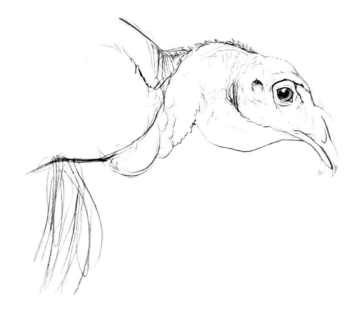

Turkey
Meleagris gallopavo
North America
Pencil drawing
approximately 4½" x 5½"

mainly for the experience, and Geoffrey O'Connell, an Ithaca boy well-known to Fuertes as a young naturalist and outdoorsman. Fuertes addressed all his letters to his wife.

Colombia, Jan. 26, 1913

It is just three weeks to-day since we left Ithaca, and it seems three months. We are still only a little more than half way up the Magdalena! . . . The nights are hot, and mosquitoes dreadful. To my great disgust, my net is too coarse, and about twenty force through every night, and I find them hanging like fat sausages to the top in the morning.

The river is fairly high, though falling slowly, and we shall have no trouble getting up to La Dorada. The crocodiles are as plenty as ever, and day before yesterday I went into the woods while we were tied up, and thought I saw a big red squirrel in a big tree. As they are "desirable" I got up closer and popped my glass on it, and it was the hind leg of a big monkey. There were four of them; an old whaling big male, the mother, and two youngsters. They were red howlers and I didn't disturb them, partly, I guess, because I had no shot that would kill them, but instead watched them for quite a while with the glasses—a fine time was had by all! At Magangué, three days ago, they brought aboard in a cage a magnificent old male jaguar—a truly royal beast. He turned out to be part of a show, a performing animal, but nevertheless a native, and a beauty.

The eastern Andes came into view the third day, after we had had a superb view, all unexpected, of the

Santa Marta mountains, snow and all! The fourth day we saw the central Andes, and have been between them ever since, though to-day the valley is so wide that neither is in view, and the river is sometimes a mile or more wide, the channels running in queer directions, between islands. . . .

Looking out just now, I see the forest half a mile back, then nearer, a broad savannah. Then a shallow stretch of shining water, and about 200 feet away a flat sandy bar in the river. On it are nine crocodiles—three big ones—and among those on one end about fifty dozing black skimmers, and over the whole thing, and quite near, floats on spread wings and in the glaring light, a beautiful pink roseate spoonbill.

Honda, 5½° N. Lat., Feb. 3, 1913

Yesterday I went out over a well-remembered trail, and had a bully time getting into the old places. But I followed it up much farther, and got some fine things way up at the head of the stream, in a deep high pocket in the mountainside, with deep and tangled forest in a perfect chaos of rocks and stream-cut gulches. Got a pair of beautiful big motmots—the biggest kind, green and blue, with the whole chest, neck and head bright chestnut red, with the big black face-marks and a black tassel in the throat. . . .

There was a fine large brawl yesterday right in front of the hotel, a running, free for all riotous, yelling, clubbing fight between some 6 mounted vaqueros—cowboys—and the general public. It lasted about 10 minutes and moved about 100 yards in that time and nobody was hurt—but the sound and sight were such

Puerto Rican Tanager
Nesospingus speculiferus
Puerto Rico
Wash drawing
approximately 5" x 7"

as to satisfy the most doggy. I never saw such moving rage in my life and wouldn't much care if I never did again. But those fellows could ride—how they could ride. . . .

Monte Redondo, Feb. 28, 1913
I shall start this now, after a hard day of hunting and skinning (h. from 6:30 to 12 on [steep] slopes; sk. from 12:45 to 6 without leaving my chair). Got one or two fine things, but not much.

Tom and I left Bogotá Sunday, the 23rd. . . .

We went over the clammy paramos of Bogotá about 5 hours' ride and got to Chipaque. There Tom and I stayed 2 days to work while Frank, Cherrie and Jeff went on to Quintame to prospect. Quintame was little good and when Tom and I caught up there with the others we only spent the night there and then hired a passing empty mule (2 of ours having slight saddle sores) packed all our stuff and walked 3 stiff mountain hours to this place, Monte Redondo; a hard long day's go, from the place we shall really settle and work hard at.

I think really that B[ogotá] was a great disappointment to us all. We had, I suppose, expected too much. Many things very interesting, but such horrible isolation can't help retarding progress except for mule-cars and el[ectric] lights and a dash of plumbing, Bogotá is as mediaeval a place as I *ever* saw, where life is discussed in little companies on the narrow, cobbled dirty streets by 16th century Spanish gentlemen, whose legs are the while brushed by loathsome, whining leprous beggars they never think of. The

papers, 1 sheet "periodicos," are filled thus: 1 column, impressions of travel (to Honda) by a subscriber; 1 column, Poems to Nature, to Inspiration, to Photography!!, etc.; 2 columns hot-incendiary editorials calling the papers and their views things you, dear, know not of. . . . It is all discussed by the lazy businessless men on the streets. You never know where you are at or how soon some hot-brained, young, self-supposed handsome and important orator will have a yelling, murder-doing-mob of 1st family's sons, barbers, peons, and drunken idlers throwing rocks at your Embassy.

I had to spend nearly twelve days [in Bogotá] . . . mostly lost time though I was only sick three days; so I lifted my head and yapped with joy like a setter pup with the hedgehog quills at last taken out of his fool chops, when last Sunday I got on the commander's bridge of a short snuff-colored mule and heard his little shoeless hoofs click under me. So far, over seven weeks gone, only 135 birds. Four weeks more to work in; got to do some collecting, and what's more, find some country, if the trip is to pan out anything like the last one. The eastern slopes are barren, treeless, hopeless, sad—and gosh how steep! For days and days, coming this journey, we've gone along little scratches on the mountains' flanks, where turkey buzzards looked like flies above us, and like other flies right straight below us. Such mountains I have never seen. Down, 2,000 or 3,000 feet so nearly under you, as you look off your sleepy ambling mule, that it makes even me gug to do it, a big river, roaring and white, lies as silent and characterless as a kink of thread on the carpet. The brown, wrinkled shoulders of the upper

Black-crowned Night Heron
Nycticorax nycticorax
Worldwide
Wash drawing
approximately 3½" x 2⅜"

American Bittern
Botaurus lentiginosus
North America
Wash drawing
approximately 9" x 7"

---

slopes rise, rise—get distantly green where the ever-lasting clouds hang and make the lofty fog-forest. Along the trails rare little farms, built so steep that they look like maps of farms tacked on the walls, harbor and faintly nourish a scattered people; the poorest, in every conceivable sense, I think, in the world. They know—of nothing, truly. They can hardly think at all, and stand in a blurry daze while you pass them, and probably for hours after. I have never been so touched by what man, God's creature, will do and do without, to live bare life, as here in these sad, huge, resourceless desolations of the eastern Andes. And I nearly cried, after thinking these and kindred thoughts, when the *wife of the hotel-keeper* in Chipaque (a town with a Plaza, fountain, a fine church [clock] that strikes by itself every fifteen minutes) said to me the last night we were there, after Tom had strung, tuned, and played the twenty-year old and still sweet guitar of the house: "Ai, senor, la vida aquí está muy triste"—"Ah, Sir, life here is very sad." Great God—what must these poor devils feel and think who in *all their lives* can never climb out of the eternal hole, heaven-high and hell-deep, in which their poor bug lives were chucked, and who have never, I almost really believe, seen another face, or cow, or pig, or any darn thing, but their own. It got my goat, and I here confess it. And I'm not such hell on my poor fellow-man, either. This is sure a *different* country. I'd like to (no, I wouldn't, but I *could*) hang myself up in its lost corners, for a year or so, and come out with a book that would make people sit up and yell! I have never seen such contrasts of people, of places, of natures and of nature. I must either have

been asleep before, or else I was in the wrong places. But I've had sensations that would just pick me up by the neck and shake out the gasps!

For instance: Last night, when we were all here, and settled in the big room "at our service" the young woman asked us if we would like some music. Certainly, what? Well, her brother had picked up the art of playing the guitar, and sang. We hadn't seen any men around that looked like her brother, so: "How old is your brother, senorita?" "He's just gone five." Well, a little somewhat old-looking babyish boy was produced in a minute. She sat in a corner and held the guitar, on her lap. The youngster stood beside her, and played, all on the neck of the guitar. He couldn't reach around it, so his thumb was only a nuisance to him, and he did the bass string with his little finger—never mind. I've heard the best "tiple" player in Bogotá, and perhaps a hundred others along the streets; this little kid played with *perfect* precision, and had all the tricks of mute, and thumb, and hush and three fingers four time (that makes your whole insides dance with them) that any I ever heard could handle. Then he sang. Madge, I would have given anything in this world to have had you (just for that hour, if you'd wished it) in this high square bare mud-floored room, lit by a candle, to see and hear the group of two in the corner. The girl was just setting. That youngster—two years younger even than Sum [his son] —sang songs, to the most moving and wild accompaniments, that were such perfect embodiment of romance that words were useless (although he had 'em) and not one but was the purest, most intensely character-istic expression of these places and people you could

Mallard
Anas platyrhynchos
Holarctic
Wash drawing
approximately 6" x 9"

possibly get. He had a curious trick of hushing then singing out like a purple finch, with his head back, everything rich minor except for an occasional line— for a question—in the major. Then that goat-getting hush on the minor reply. His sister said she had helped him with the words, *only.* He isn't a bit abnormal other ways, and when I set and baited a rat-trap in the corner he was in and out every three minutes the rest of to-day. But he is a *real* and certainly spontaneous musical prodigy, and should study—as she says he will. He sings with utter self-forgetfulness, with the open tremulous manner of these people, but there was something in his tiny youth, five years, three of which were mostly unconscious, and producing, *in spite of this battering isolation,* and never having been off this ten acres, a moving, powerful musical force like that.

I didn't know here, either, whether to laugh or cry, and was near to both. He got *all* our change, which he solemnly looked over, and then picked out all the little ones and gave them to his sister! She laughed too hard, and I suspect she was touched rather roughly. The thing is so much bigger than the kid; how in thunder did it get in him? . . .

I started this, Madgie, with two candles, ten inches long. I now have one candle, one inch long. The question is, can I get to bed (some stunt!) before I don't have any candle any inches long?

VRMMMMMMMM *** From somewhere out in the dark just then came a sawmill-like hum, and *Bat,* right on the side of the head, with a fine chill-bringing crescendo, landed a thing like an elephantine junebug with a[monstrous]head:h'raus mit 'em. I jumped clear across the room. Candle now [low]. This can't go on,

for I can't hold the bug any longer, nor let go indoors —good-night, more later.

Monday P.M. at Buena Vista, 90 miles S.E. of Bogotá
We went out early next a.m., and up a trail-less mountainside pasture, up, up, to reach some cloud forest that crawls over the top of the range and drops in festoons down into the valley-heads. We got there, separately, and met. I was sprawled on the stones at the edge of the little stream, my cork so pulled that Tom said afterward I didn't talk sense. Be that as it may, for once in my life I had nothing left, and had to quit at my goal, for I couldn't go another rod. I sat in the sun in a little manioca patch right there for an hour taking frequent drinks from the stream, and then, Tom having gone on up into the forest (a mighty stunt of vigor and nerve, for he was all but as gone as I), I picked a laborious and exhausting way down the stream-bed to a "water-trail" where they divert a small stream to carry miles through fields and farms, for domestic use in distant *posadas,* etc. Then it was easy, for there's always an up-keep path. I got back to Monte Redondo (only one house, a *posado* along the trail) about 11, changed clo' and rested till 12, asleep most of the time, and was fit as a fiddle again by noon. Manuel had in the meantime returned from Bogotá, with the news that Paul is still sick and can't move for another week, and to cap it all, he had the mail for the crowd, and after waiting all this time, not a thing for me. I can't tell you, possibly, how hurt and disappointed I was. . . .

Well, we left Monte Redondo the next morning at

Pintail
Anas acuta
Holarctic
Wash drawing
approximately 7" x 5"

seven on our mules that were sent up from B. Vista and arrived the previous p.m. We passed all morning, like flies along an elephant's belly, along the steep flank of bare or grass-covered mountains. We made an all day ride of it....

To the other side (and you only have to turn in your tracks, as we're on a narrow ridge) you look down and up into valleys and ranges, numberless, of richly forested mountains, towering away, bluer and bluer till you see "beetling crags" of pale sapphire apparently resting on fleecy pinky white cottony clouds. At 5:30 to 5:45 in the evening, the sunset takes place in the lowest V formed by interlacing ranges, and I can't begin to give you any idea of the glory. This is a different country from any we have seen, and most miraculously beautiful; but its chief interest to us is that it brings *down* cloud-forest forms—of plants and birds both—and brings up Orinoco and Amazonian life to meet them. As an example: we went out, the five of us, this a.m., and brought in between us about 70 specimens of birds. This number represented about 42 species, and 38 *genera!!* We hardly had in the whole bag a species that was taken yesterday. I got *two* of my wonderful whistling birds—a slightly different species, but essentially the same thing—an enormous toucan, a fine dark-forest hummer, etc.

The forests are superb. There is a June-like climate, *no* mosquitoes nor flies, no dripping burning perspiration, just cool lovely pestless collecting, in enormous dry floored forest. There are a number of trails leading through it, and you can go silently through aisles of gigantic trees and rich middle growth with profusion of hanging lianas and parasites. (Incidentally,

we saw yesterday, growing *wild* in the forest, great sprays of the "dollar apiece" lavender orchids.) If you hear something off the trail, it is open enough to work easily through in any direction. I criss-crossed the ridge beyond to-day in any old direction. Perfectly ideal collecting, in the richest fauna I have even seen, and to me, *all new.*

Villavicencio, Mar. 12, 1913

At last—at last! Yesterday Paul turned up from Bogotá (having made the whole journey in three days —*good* going for a sick man) and brought me your first three letters. You will never know the joy of getting them. A mail goes to Bogotá from here Saturday the fifteenth and this will go by it, and take chances from B. down the river....

Since I wrote you from Monte Redondo, where Tom and I were temporarily stranded, the party has relayed along the trail, stopping at favorable places....

With the exception of three baddish days in Bogotá early in Feb. my health has been beyond reproach. I have been careful not to overtax myself and have been absogoshdurnlutely all right, eating 3 squares a day, and tearing off the sleep stuff at about 9–12 hours per night. To date I have just 222 birds and am getting about 12–15 a day. This is the busiest season we've had, for we are right in a rich field and six men at it every day. I paint one or two things almost every day, for somebody gets something I can't refuse almost daily. Then skin till supper and maybe after—and to bed a dead dog....

This morning I spent nearly an hour in a perfectly

Shovelers
Spatula clypeata
Holarctic
Wash drawing
approximately 13" x 8½"

Short-billed Dowitchers
Limnodromus griseus
North America
Pencil drawing
approximately 3" x 5"

hellish thicket of weeds, about ten feet high and so thick I couldn't see five feet in any direction, and bearing the damnedest little burrs, in millions, that ever drew curse from human throat—so big ∗ , and just long-pointed enough to prick and itch through such clothes as I wear. The bush has also thorns, or rather hooks. While in the midst of a most exciting still hunt (imagine it in such a place) for the author of an easily imitable bird whistle, my already burr-covered cap stuck and came off, and I turned my head in reaching back for it and got "about a thousan" in my poor hair!! Before I was done in there I was so mad I could have cried; sweating like a July ice-pitcher (only feeling different), prodded and pricked at every turn, I called that little bird up to within probably fifteen feet three times—when he'd get wise without my having seen him at all and *run* away again. Never once did he even hop up on a stick. A mouse is a moose compared to the slick action of this thing. Finally, as a last resort, I tried a trick on him. I bulled my way, regardless of him, to a place where, in a low wettish spot, I could by squatting, see spots of ground for twenty-five or thirty feet around. Then I called again, and in about five minutes got an answer from perhaps 100 feet away. I pulled him up to about 50 and then, instead of doing it full strength I did it softly in the same key, hoping he might think I was further away. And it *worked!* Immediately it came from only about half the distance; I sat tight and burned holes through the burr-bush with my eyes for the tail of a motion—or the motion of a tail—and was rewarded by seeing a ghost of a shadow move along a rotten branch. The direction seemed just right, and I popped my Aux at

it and went in (it took five minutes to get thirty feet) and there lay the slickest little long-legged, stub-tailed, Jersey-cow eyed little shadow-bird you ever saw. It is a *grallaria,* related to my "whistle" bird of Miraflores, but a little species I have never seen. So, just 45 minutes after I began, I came out with the prize bird of the day (and trip, no doubt) though to-day's lot included a *fancy* pigeon, one of the finest of the family, a new type of forest-dove, most lovely, and a little pale *blue* ground dove, with a black tail and a white head and neck, and trimmed with round black velvet spangles on his wings.

This stuff I did not intend to shove at you, but it got out just ahead of me. We all continue well, and I want to tell you that I can't get up to Bogotá any too soon for me, for I shall probably find another letter or two from you.

Good night, Madge dear, and my best and only love to you and the children; how I'll come running when at last the downhill trip begins—about two weeks more afield and then "All aboard for Alabam."

(Naught was heard but the raucous scratch, scratch of Geoff, in his sleep.)

Your loving,
Louis

Bogotá, Colombia, Mar. 21, 1913
Good Friday!
We're off again in the morning at 7, for Fusugasugá, some thirty miles S.W. of here, for the rest of our time —some two weeks.

Since my last note, Jeff and I have had an experi-

Louis Agassiz Fuertes

Green-winged Teal
Anas carolinensis
North America
Pencil drawing
approximately 2¼" x 4"

ence, which I will have fun telling you about when I get home. It was the funniest, and at the same time the most uncomfortable two days and nights ('specially nights) I ever had. We stopped, and left the rest to go on to Bogotá, at a little lonesome *posada* or road house way up on the *paramo,* at 10,600 feet. It was cold and raw when we got there, about 3:30 p.m. Tuesday 18th, and a wet fog was blowing through the pass, only one and a half miles away, and the people—poor as dirt and covered with it—didn't want to take us in for a cent. Only Cherrie's smiles and diplomacy, and the fact that we took off our packs and sent the mules on with the others, made them take us.

It was too cold and raw to hunt, and we couldn't see through the fog anyway. So we stuck around the place and got acquainted with our quarters. Quarters is the word, for they assigned us to a low platform in one corner of the one room in the shack—a mud affair with a bunch-grass thatch, no windows (thank God!) and one door: mud floor and mud everywhere else. We (and they) had no candles, so after dusk, when it settled down to be real cold, there was nothing for it but bed. So we put down our blow beds, fixed our blankets, and threw and pinned an extra double blanket over both beds, and taking off only sweaters and shoes, got in and passed a fair night.

We had had cocoa and native soup for "dinner." Later, all the family, consisting of father, mother, some old female relation, two younger women, several youths, a little girl about eight, and an utterly, bitterly, putrescently filthy brat of two—innocent since birth of any cleansing influence—all crawled into a sort of hole in the farther wall for the night, where they snored, hawked, etc., etc., till dawn, when they crawled sniffling and coughing out into the chilly fog for wet firewood, and the day began. We had cocoa again, and went out to hunt. Bitter business: *paramo* dripping, clouds driving drizzle, and birds as tight as Jamaica ticks to their hiding places. We got a few, and got in at noon. Dinner: potato soup, wheat soup, cocoa. Skinned birds, after a change and a rub, till it got so bloody cold we couldn't make our hands track. I spoiled three good hummers straight, because I shook so. Poor Jeff never stopped shivering from the time we got there till we left. But he put out a line of hopeless traps, just the same, like a man. It hailed in the afternoon, just lending the final touch of penetration to the cold. That night we had for supper potato soup, potatoes, and a little rice.

Early to bed with numb feet, that staid so till we left. But before we turned in a pair of sad old pack-horses of women came in off the trail. They couldn't be turned out on the *paramo* at night (murder, no less) so they were shown into the room. They had a taller-dip, and made a pretty picture from our beds, lousing each other in the candle-light with claw-like hands, and grunting, snuffling, and hawking in the cold against the flickering background of smoked mud walls, their witchlike shadows dancing with the jumping light. But this time the dogs and cat and one of the turkeys were all in *the* room, and after the family had crawled into their den, and the "padron" had *tied* on the door for the night, we were all ready for a real cozy night, laughing and talking until a late hour.

The poor old dames grunted into their packs and shuffled out in the cold dawn. A roaring east wind,

Black-capped Mocking Thrush
Donacobius atricapille
Central and South America
Wash drawing
approximately 9" x 7"

the sign of the rains, had sprung up, and the bare *paramos* whistled with it, and the thick black soaking fog slid over the pass and isolated us in a very short time after light. We knew we had eaten nearly everything they had, and that to hunt in this was out of the question, so, as temporary head of the exped., I told Jeff to go get his traps, hired the old man to take our packs to Bogotá on his mule, got breakfast started, packed up our outfit, and after breakfast started afoot with the howling wind behind us, for Bogotá. The breakfast deserves mention. First, cocoa. Then, a half hour later, a plate of soup, potato variety. Second course, soup—pomme de terre—overture by the donkey, to show breakfast was over.

So we got out—and just then the clouds broke and out came the sun! But we were packed and couldn't re-arrange in time to do anything, so we kept on, and had only been on the road three quarters of an hour when we met our boy, Manuel, with two saddle mules and a pack mule, sent up for us by Chapman, who had *just* got to the hotel in Bogotá Tuesday when the fever hit him. Rotten luck, but pretty fortunate not to get caught on the road. He hadn't a very high fever, but last night he had a beast of a chill, that absolutely exhausted him. . . .

It is 11:30—wildly late—and our packs leave at 6. and we at 7.—so good night.

Your own,
Louis

Bogotá, Colombia, April 9, 1913
. . . The expedition has collected over 2,000 birds besides my 400 or more, and we have a very represen-

tative lot. Six men turned loose in a locality for a few days nearly cleans up the list of representative species. I doubt if any collection of 2,400 birds ever contained so many species, and little Rollo has just about everything that is of particular interest or that he didn't have before.

Barranquilla, Colombia, April 17, 1913
Beginning where I left off in my last from Bogotá, Cherrie, Jeff and I took the mules down from Facatativá to Honda over the old trail we came up three months back, and got as far as El Consuelo, where we expected to spend the night, about 4 p.m. Here we found a special message from F.M.C. that if possible we were to come right through, for he had decided to take the "express" boat from Honda next day at 9:30, so as to catch a Hamburg-Am. steamer for N.Y. Thursday. (That was Saturday.) So, though it's a six-hour ride from El C. to Honda, and the rains were on, we slid right along, and after a really pretty bad ride through the mountains in the pitch dark—letting the mules pick their way, and with a tropical thunderstorm brewing about us and blinding us occasionally with its fireworks—we at last got to H. at about 8:45, to our and others' great relief. Manuel, who was behind us, got the word we had left for him at Consuelo, and pushed on with the packs, and got in, drenched and a little frightened and excited, at just midnight. We got the express all right, with everything—twenty clothes boxes, two trunks and two big packing boxes of birds included—right with us; good business, as it's the entire collection. My share is almost exactly

Pyrrhuloxia
Pyrrhuloxia sinuata
Southwest United States
Wash drawing
approximately 3" x 2"

400 birds, it would have been just except that I lost the little basket containing the few we collected on our Facatativá-Honda trip off my saddle in the dark, near Honda.

In Bogotá, the last day, I found and bought the biggest and most perfectly gorgeous jaguar skin I ever saw. I'll have it tanned in N.Y. first and then sent up. . . .

Well, dear child, I'll be with you in a couple of days after this reaches you. My love to you, dear, and the kids.

Louis

Field Museum of Natural History and *Chicago Daily News* Expedition to Abyssinia, 1926-1927

By 1926, Fuertes had not undertaken a major collecting expedition since his Colombia trip with Chapman in 1913. During these years he lived quietly with his family in Ithaca, painting very actively and serving, from 1923 to 1927, as a resident lecturer at Cornell, a post he accepted after he turned down a professorship. Some of his important work of the period was done for the National Geographic Magazine, for which he illustrated not only several articles on birds but also pieces on North American mammals and dogs.

On a summer trip to Wyoming, in 1925, Fuertes met James E. Baum, a sportsman and writer. Baum was planning a three-month hunt in Abyssinia—"the strangest country in the world to-day"—and proposed that Fuertes accompany him. This was to be an expedition unlike any Fuertes had taken before. "Modest" is the word that applies to the earlier ones, except for the Harriman expedition, and in that Fuertes had been a minor figure. Now he was to be the star of an expedition which had adequate if not lavish financial support, which would receive much publicity—almost daily bulletins in some newspapers—and which would bring him to the court of Ras Tafari (Haile Selassie), heir to the throne of Ethiopia (Abyssinia).

Baum hoped to get credentials from the Field Museum of Natural History in Chicago, and he and Fuertes visited Wilfred Hudson Osgood, curator of zoology at the Field Museum and a close friend of Fuertes for thirty years. Osgood raised the proposal to a higher level by talking to Stanley Field, president of the museum. From this point on, said Osgood to Fuertes, "you'd better relinquish all idea of doing this

stunt in a small way." Fuertes was now involved with the director and trustees of the museum and with shaping matters of policy for the journey.

Baum took off on another tack and soon had great success. He sent a telegram to Fuertes on April 16: "Everything arranged stop [Chicago Daily] News will finance whole expedition to the extent of twenty-five thousand hooray." Baum had agreed to keep a record of the expedition's activities, sending it back in installments for the newspaper.

By April 19, Osgood had committed himself fully to the idea of getting outside support. No more, he said, "of the old Biol. Survey days ... and a starvation allowance." He had come to terms with those who saw the place of publicity in expeditions of this sort. "I've lost all conscience, modesty, prof. ethics, etc., and if publicity gets results and especially if a newspaper is our patron, I'm for seeking their end of it as well as ours." It was a time of enthusiastic and far-ranging journeys dedicated to the study of nature. Theodore Roosevelt, Jr., and Kermit Roosevelt had just returned from a trip in search of the vanished Ovis poli, Marco Polo's sheep; William Beebe of the New York Zoological Society had played up his work on the Sargasso Sea; Roy Chapman Andrews of the American Museum was off in search of dinosaur eggs. "Gosh," concluded Osgood, "if we can do no better, I'm for the good old Queen of Sheba."

Preparations went forward quickly and steadily through the summer. Mary, Fuertes' daughter, sailed in midsummer for a trip to Europe. Fuertes traveled with his wife as far as France so that she might keep Mary and a friend of hers, Barbara Wyckoff, com-

Common Tern
Sterna hirundo
North America
Pencil drawing
approximately 9" x 7"

pany during the winter that he was in Africa. Thus almost all his letters to his family were written to France.

Fuertes' mother stayed in the United States, as did his sister, Katherine. Fuertes therefore had a news-writing problem. He solved it by writing a general news letter with one or two carbon copies, then making appropriate additional notes for the individual recipients.

The expedition staff consisted of Fuertes, Wilfred Hudson Osgood, Jack Baum, Alfred M. Bailey, a young zoologist, and C. Suydam Cutting, an amateur naturalist and sportsman. Cutting helped finance the portfolio Album of Abyssinian Birds and Mammals, *which was published in 1930 and contained about half the water colors Fuertes completed during the expedition. In the opinion of Frank Chapman this was the finest work Fuertes did.*

About 3/4 down the Red Sea, Oct. 3, 1926.
Dear ones on land—Pos. hot, Compar. hotter, Sup. hottest. Life is one B.V.D. after another, with a splash of Red Sea water between...

But for the birds that are apt to turn up any minute it would be exceedingly dull. The old Red Sea is 1,300 miles long, and it seems interminable. With luck we'll get to Jibuti about 4 p.m. tomorrow, and have two days there before the Wednesday train goes up to Addis.

We came through most of the canal at night, but in the early a.m. were still in the Bitter Lakes which form its middle, and as it narrowed saw many herons, cranes, hawks, some bright little jewel-like kingfishers (sparrow size), and—best of all—three flamingos were feeding only about 200 yards from the boat, and didn't fly or seem at all disturbed, and gave us a great thrill. Since leaving Suez we've been continually out of sight of land, but almost always swallows, wagtails, wheat-ears, kestrels, terns, or a fine big dark eagle with the whole crown and nape cream white have been about the ship. This a.m. half a dozen tiny migrant quail, half or less the size of our bobwhite, have been wearily following us, lighting occasionally on the deck or awnings, and getting chased off before they caught their breath. Yesterday we had four kestrels (a small falcon) and at one time four eagles sailing about in the wake. Three of the k[estrel]s spent the night aboard and are still with us. They are holding high mass on the after deck, singing and intoning— we've a score of priests and nuns aboard—and I'm in disgrace at the other end of the ship, but not quite alone. There are other unregenerates aboard too.

Addis Ababa, Oct. 8, 1926
At last we're here, after a most wonderful journey. You know that the endless Red Sea was hot, and we were all intensely relieved to get to Jibuti, especially after the ship's gang had all gone back on board. We had 2½ days there, and none too much to get the baggage and transportation muddles unmuddled and see the place. The last afternoon Bailey and I hired a terrible old hack and a little rat of an old horse and went out to Ambouli, an oasis two or three miles from Jibuti, and in less than an hour I had collected seven-

Chestnut-crowned Antpitta
Grailaria (Hypsebemon) ruficapilla
South America
Wash drawing
approximately 6" x 4½"

teen birds with my pistol, every one of which we skinned and put up before going to bed; a good job.

Early Wed. a.m. the train pulled out for Addis, with all five of us sumptuously established in the Salon car by ourselves. All a.m. we passed through Somali country, saw many dik-diks—slender little antelopes not larger than rabbits—most engaging little things that dash away for a few rods and then stop and look back over their shoulders. Tall grass hides them!

It would take a week to tell you all the things we've seen. We spent the first night at Dirredawa, where it was hot, being only 2,000 ft. or so; the second at Awash, where the R.R. crosses the river; the third day, to-day, brought us to Addis Ababa, up on the plateau of 8,000 ft., where it is cool and lovely. Last night (this is the a.m. of the 8th) the thermo. registered a low of 48°, and sleeping was intense and delicious after the two weeks straight of hot nights.

There is no describing Addis, so I'll try! Crowded aimless streets—full of people of all sorts, cattle, sheep, goats, camels, horses, burros, and more of the same. Our auto journey to the British Embassy was a triumphal procession, honk-honking every second, going at 1st or 2nd speed, parting the throngs, in which the panic is equally enjoyed by all the various elements therein.

The hotel is a great rambling place with huge high rooms, a lovely garden all around, several yards and outbuildings on the slope behind. At 6:30 kites, crows, a big white-bibbed crow, a great thick-billed raven with a white nape, a stumpy-tailed small crow, and a couple of huge vultures were all around. When a servant left the hotel with a tray he carried a knife which he waved over his head, in spite of which a kite swooped down and tried to snitch the food from the tray!

Coming across the plain a harrier (marsh hawk) sprung a quail and it dropped to earth to hide; the hawk dropped too, *chased* it out of the grass, but the quail got off to a quicker start and pulled away, on which the harrier quit and flew off. But a small falcon had seen the whole business, and instantly wheeled, *doubled* his speed, and hauled the quail down in less than 100 yards, picked it right out of the air as neatly as you please and carried it off. This all happened in say 10 or 15 seconds, but the action was all parallel to us only a few rods away, and was seen by all five of us. Five minutes later we saw two lanner falcons try to catch a swallow, but they weren't good enough and a timely twist at the last moment put the swallow twenty yards out of the line—more than the hawks thought worth diving over....

Our first night was too weird and eerie for words. It gets dark soon after sunset, so when we finished dinner and came up it was pitch black. An old crone was working by a lantern on one side, her great black shadow chasing all over the white wall behind her; across the court a servant was watching his master's horse, also by lantern light, and singing the wildest queerest minor Midway chant you ever heard, full of quirks and quavers, now falsetto and now down an octave or two....

I "wished you was with us" all the way from Jibuti to Addis; the Red Sea would have killed you off. We saw more beautiful things than I ever saw before in my life, and I wonder what kind of eyes and minds

White-faced Ibis
Plegadis chihi
Southwestern United States, Central America,
South America
Pencil drawing
approximately 3" x 5"

the people have who say that it is a dull desert trip, hot and uninteresting. It beats anything I ever saw, and I wouldn't have missed a mile of it for anything. The long slim straight black Somalis, in rags and a long spear, and a hellish knife stuck in their belts—then the Danakils, not very different but usually with a rhino-hide shield, watching sheep, herding cattle or goats, leading long strings of tawny camels—*always* armed with spear and knife, were in themselves enough to make you glad you were here, they are so different from *anything* you ever saw before.

[To Mary]

Addis Ababa
[Oct. 8–11(?), 1926]

Here are your little friends the dik-diks, with some of the other beasties and birdses that gladden the eye when plastered on the landscape extending from Ji-buti to Awash—from sea level to say 5,000 ft.

You would have loved every queer sight and sound not to say smell (or aroma) that percolated to our avid senses—of all of which there were many—all new.

This (or these) are probably the longest letters I'll have a chance to write for many a day, as we are just now marking time till the arrival (through customs) of our outfit at the hotel, when serious and arduous work commences. Then first you know we'll be up and at 'em. By the time you read these lines, we should be in camp in the alluring Arusi country, on the trail of the wily nyala and etc. . . .

Your much excited and
anticipatory Dad.

Addis Ababa, Oct. 11, 1926

We rec'd word this a.m. that we were to meet at the British Legation at 3:30 to go with the *chargé,* Mr. McLean, and have our audience with the Ras Tafari [Haile Selassie, the present Emperor of Ethiopia] at 4. So we hired the hotel's two cars, put on clean collars and started off. It was really a most interesting thing. The audience was held in a small room at the Queen's palace, not Ras T's own throne room, and was rather democratic, though formal and austere at first. His Highness was only accompanied by his own personal waiting man. There were the five of us, the British *chargé,* an interpreter, and the Ras's little silky brown dog. The lion was in a big cage outside, having outgrown the throne steps.

Osgood was presented, and he introduced each of us in turn. The Ras shook hands warmly, and smiled, but said nothing. He sat down, and we did, and after a little pause smiled at O., who started in in English, and through the interpreter outlined our plans, expressed the amenities, and did a very good job. We all felt that we had been cordially received, and that the Ras was interested.

Personally, he is the color of very old ivory, with black close curled hair, beard, and moustache. Black eyes, large, expressive, but tired-looking; his face perfectly non-committal till something pleases him, when it breaks into a most engaging and friendly smile. One feels that he doesn't get too many chances to use it, though. He is about 36, slight, not tall; I doubt if he weighs 130. He was not dressed differently from any other well-born Abyssinian—black burnoose over white shama and trousers, very nice French shoes. He

Pileated Woodpecker
Dryocopus pileatus
North America
Pencil drawing
approximately 7" x 9"

has slender, soft, but very firm hands, like a painter's ought to be. There was no Oriental flurry nor pomp. While there were hundreds and hundreds of civilian retainers all over the place, we didn't see an armed guard anywhere....

One piece of bad luck thus far has fallen on me, for when we came to check up on our outfit, neither of my pieces—the trunk nor the duffle bag—were among them. The probability is that they got side-tracked in New York and have never been sent at all, though Cutting says they were there before his, and I had receipts before I left Ithaca. It is pretty tough, but doesn't wreck anything except my painting. Clothes I can get, blankets and beds are furnished, tools are in duplicate, and guns also. But I am handicapped by having to use untried and unaccustomed tools, inadequate clothes for the uplands where it gets really cold, no painting nor even drawing things at all, and the loss of a whole trunkful of conveniences—drying trays, skinning tools, etc., that I had carefully planned. But I can get along, and it would take a lot more than that to throw me.

Addis Ababa
Oct. 17, 1926

... The State dinner was marvelous, and we all enjoyed it hugely. We were the last to arrive—just on the dot. The British *chargé* and wife, all the American Hospital crowd, two Americans who trek west tomorrow, the Belgian Minister and wife, a Belgian consul from Dirredawa and wife, the French Minister, and ourselves. A plan of the seating was on a table; I'll have to describe the rooms later. Snifters were served by black Abyssinians in white dress suits, gold buttons and skin tight trow. Bare feet, for once, were not in evidence, of course. After the amenities, we were shown into a large brightly lighted reception room, and the line proceeded to the far end, where Ras Tafari, in white with a close-collared long cape of deepest purple, with a gold throat-latch, stood beside his large and dusky consort, dressed in white soft cotton embroidered *à la* Maya. This part was very formal and whispery, and as soon as everybody had been received and passed on, with only the briefest pause, the Ras led off very slowly and, ladies first, we all filed into the state dining hall. An imposing room, with modern pictures (hunting scenes were pronounced Old Baltimore Rye ads by Cutting), a long table with solid goldfish and gold service, no kid, and cut glass in half dozen for each. The Ras sat in the middle of one side, the consortina opposite, and the conventional black concentrated at the ends.

The food was marvelous, a most ingenious mixture of European dishes with native confections, three kinds of wine—red, white, champagne—and—*tej*. The latter was the first we have experienced, and wasn't s'much. It is usually milky buff-colored stuff in old jars or dirty bottles with a bunch of leaves stuck in for a cork, and plumb unintriguing. It was a "clear amber liquid," tasting a little burned or smoky. We all tasted it and smiled appreciatively, with loathing in our hearts. I raised my glass to the Ras's son-in-law, who knows no word of European talk, and he smiled a luminous smile and lifted his champagne glass—which was a relief, because I could change and did....

Yours till I return, anyway.

Dovekie
Plautus alle
North Atlantic
Wash and pencil drawing
approximately 9" x 7"

Bay-breasted Warbler
Dendroica castanea
North America
Wash drawing
approximately 2½" x 2½"

Thurs. Oct. 21, '26
Col. Sandford's farm on the Muger River,
35 mi. north of Addis Ababa

Monday, Bailey and I rode over here, with a change of horses, over the Entoto hills (10,000 ft.) and across the great savannah of the plateau. Great cranes, herons, three kinds of ibis, two of geese, and countless small birds abounded. I had my pistol handy, and collected 17 birds on the ride, four of which were none other than the mysterious horned lark *(Otocoris poli)* himself! That, you will remember, is the bird-objective of the trip (I now have six) being represented [in the United States] by a single specimen marked only "Africa."

We got here very tired, at about 2:30, and as soon as we got partly rested were called to tea! Fresh cake, and fresh (don't faint) strawberries and cream! We were soon bucked up, and I got most of my birds skinned before dark. . . .

Just now we are working very hard, as this is only a brief opportunity. . . . Up at daylight, dawn, rather, and on the trail by 6 or 6:15. By 9:30 or 10 we've covered several miles, each on his own hunch, and are back at the house with an all day and evening's job. A silent, good-natured Galla boy follows our every step, and carries not only our game and an extra gun, but a basket of fresh strawberries: tough, *I* calls it!

Each day is jammed full of thrill and discovery. To-day I shot a most beautiful little eagle, all pale rich tan with heavily black and gray barred wings and tail, and a full soft crest on his nape. He was very lean and slender, with an awful lot of style; I never heard of one like it, nor saw a museum specimen. Those gorgeous gleaming glossy starlings are common. We sit on the porch skinning, and toss the bodies of birds and mice into the air; none has yet hit ground, for a dozen graceful kites sailing around nip them on the fly as daintily as can be. At lunch yesterday a great form slid by the window; Bailey grabbed the .22 rifle and went to the door and there on the edge of the garden sat a magnificent eagle, a true *aquila,* like our Golden (only this one was all pale buff with dark tail and primaries).

We have so much work to do that we can't stop to paw over and study the things we get. As each day's hunt gets us birds we never heard of, often of great beauty, that is rather too bad, but inevitable. . . .

Love to Mary and Babs—and I hope you are not skimping on your opportunity because the money seems to slip. I want you and Mary to get the very most of everything; another chance may never come.

Don't worry about me; I'm going like a new Ford —and I hope to do as well as an old one. Good night.

Addis Ababa, Oct. 26, 1926

All your news is good, and I don't believe wife ever told husband before that she had too much money!

. . . Except for the damn flies, which treat me here as ever, I'm having a wonderful time. I'm as hard as I've ever been, can climb and work hard all a.m. in the rocks and hillsides and skin till bed time without undue fatigue, sleep like a child and wake up pink and refreshed, at sunup, ready for the new day! Put up about 85 skins in the six days, including eleven of the *Otocoris poli,* and on the way in collected the

Dovekie

Feet

Scales on tarsi & toes milky blue-white, with sharp
black lines between. Joints more dusky, as well as
back of shank. Soles and webs of feet blackish
tongue & inside of mouth pearly pink-white

Wilson's Petrel (left)
Oceanites oceanicus
Worldwide
Leach's Petrel (right)
Oceanodroma leucorhoa
World wide
approximately 3¼" x 5"

nest and eggs!—the first ever recorded, several large hawks, etc., and Bailey got nearly the same number of mammals, including three klipspringers, and four huge baboons. So you see, we, too, have not been idle. And the stuff is all A1, no junk nor half-done jobs in the lot, either.

Mary, how you would have loved the ride in over the twenty-odd miles of savannah land. We had splendid ponies that ride like Diamond G horses, fifteen miles and then fresh ones for the last half. Sacred ibis, a black crested ibis, herons and geese let you ride almost up to them, but the most exciting are the great cranes—standing as high as the little humped cattle—that let you ride up to perhaps 50 or 60 feet before they spread their glorious black-and-white wings, drop their long necks, and "run up" the speed necessary for a take-off—trumpeting loud and long as they pick up, and with a stately rhythm fly up and up, until they can sail, like angels, if I picture them right—wheeling up and up and up into the sky till the long line of neck and legs gets lost to the eye, and they are just transverse lines wheeling in the burning blue of noon. I'd rather be able to do that than anything I ever saw done—but an ear-splitting engine would spoil it: it's the most serene thing any living thing does.

In camp, on Mt. Albasso
(10,000 ft. alt.), Nov. 12, 1926

This is the first time I have sat down to write since we left Addis, now twelve days ago. We went by train to Mojo, getting there 24 hrs. before our caravan. . . . Ever since then we have trekked, making one-night

stands, off by 8 a.m. next day, 35 men and 52 mules strong. We spelled the mules (and men) one night at the Kalata River (where I got Menelik's oriole, *inter al.*), in the Awash drainage. That was a fine wild place; hyenas yapping around and a leopard's fresh trax in the creek bed; big steel traps yielded—an eagle! Then up out of the valley and onto the southern plateau of Arusi. After a couple of longish marches we finally arrived at this beautiful place—the head of one of the many little (but very troublesome) gulches, with a small local forest, a purling stream, and square miles of grass for the animules. . . .

Yesterday, out ten days and all O.K., we bought two bullocks (a Christian one and a Mohammedan one) for the men. Last night they had a grand raw-meat feast, and to-day the camp looks like a N.Y. back area-way with all the red stockings in the world hung out to dry—rods and rods and rods of strings of "jerky" with squealing kites and great croaking thick-billed ravens swirling constantly above, not *quite* daring to snitch the meat. . . .

Here the characteristic things are ravens—great croaking buzzards with a white nape and deep heavy bill that light on the backs of sore mules and eat the raw live flesh of the poor things; eagles of several kinds, vultures, and the great "Lammergeyer," a bearded vulture, one of the largest birds in the world, and a most monstrous-fine flier; kites; a large white-breasted hawk; Bateleur eagles; on the barer parts of the hills francolins like huge quail, of two kinds, give most beautiful shooting and delicious food; doves of several kinds hoot, grunt, coo, or rattle in the boscage, according to their individual wont (or will).

Chimney Swifts
Chaetura pelagica
Eastern North America
Wash and pen and ink
approximately 9" x 6"

Of little things there are many; snap-shots at wiggles in the low bush yield new things almost daily, and several of them should prove *really* new. By far the loveliest of all are two kinds of sunbirds, tiny slender things that replace hummingbirds in this continent. One is black, resplendent with shines of purple, green, and bronze; the other is *all* rich iridescent *emerald* green (blue toward the sun) with a little fan of dandelion yellow feathers in front of each wing.

I have skinned and put up just 200 birds—almost 100 per week of being in the field. At this rate (which of course will fall as we assemble the characteristic fauna) we'll have a very big and representative collection of Abyssinian birds when we're through. We go still south from here, toward Jumm Jumm, then swing west, through the pass south of Lake Zwai (big game country) and back north to Addis Ababa. Then we'll probably take a trip north to Gojjam, in the arm of the Blue Nile, the upper heights of which have been but scantily noticed by naturalists. If our luck holds we'll certainly get a bunch of things; almost all the desired things are already in camp, O. topping it off yesterday by shooting a fine dog wolf, the peculiar red wolf of Abyssinia, *not* heretofore taken south of the rift—a really fine animal, rarer than the nyala, and even more local. This may well be an undescribed form....

I had a bit of bum luck at Mojo; an acacia branch snapped back and drove a half-inch thorn way into the back of my leg, just above my leather legging, and broke it off flush with the skin. Before I could get back to the house it had worked under and away from the hole; I dug for it, but without effect, so had to leave it.

It literally gave me hell for two or three days, as I couldn't bend a foot without pulling all the muscles crossways, and I couldn't straighten my leg without pushing it in, and hurting like the devil. But now it's O.K., and I hardly know I have it. Whether it's absorbing or what I don't know, but it's not even sore any more, for which I am truly grateful. For a while I was terribly worried lest I have to leave the ex. or hold it up, but nothing of the kind happened for which I thank Mary's little brass rabbit, which I hung on my Ingersoll strap that night!...

The sun has slipped behind the shoulder to the west, and a chill spreads instantly over everything. So I'm going to don my Zebra coat (a life-saver—*gosh* I'm glad I didn't pack it in my trunk!) and make a holler for supper....

Addis Ababa, Jan. 20, 1927
Yesterday afternoon O. and I pulled into Addis Ababa ahead of our caravan, which arrived this a.m. about 10.... We weren't looking for it much before tomorrow noon.... You will want to know of our doings so here goes. After my last letter, from old Chilalo's chilly slopes, we all hung together till Thanksgiving, parting the next day on southern Chilalo, Baum, Bailey and Cutting going s.e., to cross the Webbi Shebeli to Sheik Hussein after lions and big stuff; O. and I heading for Lajo crossing of the W.S. (s. and w.) to work the Gedeb Mts., then go down through Bale and Sidamo to Allata in the Jumm Jumm district—a type locality for a lot of Neumann's new mammals. I turned into a pretty fair rifle shot, and

Ring-necked Duck
Aythya collaris
North America
Wash drawing
approximately 18" x 26"

became head monkey-hunter, and got by with some distinction, getting eight guerezas—great black and white plumed monkeys, a fine old male of the unique jamjam monkey (known only from Neumann's type) and later a ♀, and several smaller ones of almost equal value. Besides this I painted 50 or 60 field studies, many quite elaborate, and collected and preserved 559 birds on the trip, in over 40 different camps! So you see I wasn't idle *all* the time. O. got nearly 300 mammals, including several big antelope—hartebeest, etc. "The wild hyenas round us howl'd," but we'd no adventures of a dangerous kind, and came through sound and still friends in spite of our hardening arteries and peculiarities, and are ready for more. . . .

XXX

Those x's stand for 24 hours, in which much has happened. Of course the absorbing thing is the arrival, safe and sound, on the train yesterday, of the rest of the outfit. We had a grand reunion. They also had a fine trip. . . .

I've had a few minor and innocent adventures, but mostly we've gotten by with no distracting loss of time. Our state visits to local governors, etc., were so interesting that we couldn't really grudge the time lost, except once, when, having got behind the caravan to hunt some red bee-eaters, I was haled by a small chief in passing his gibbi and held a "social" prisoner for 2 hours while he looked us up. . . .

When you write to me in Alexandria give me all the dope you can about your plans and especially where you will be about the middle and end of May, when we expect to be through here. I'd hate to have to ask Mr. Munroe [the permanent address for his wife and daughter], "Where is my wandering wife tonight?"; which is my only recourse if you don't tell me yourself. Think it over, kid.

I'm crazy to see you both and hear you talk French. After I'd conversed, as I thought fluently, in French with my captor in Wando, I was much chagrined when he said: "It surprises me that you don't speak French. Why, French is the polite language of every country, and *tout le monde* speaks French!" Can you beat that for a squash?

[To Frank M. Chapman]

Addis Ababa, Jan. 23, 1927

Osgood and I just got in two days ago from the first long leg of our trip, and I found in my letters (three months' grist of them!) your fine one of Oct. 28th. . . .

My best congratulations, *Old Man,* on being a grandfather! I had a shock myself when I let my whiskers grow out summat, to find that they are *snow white,* and I look 75 in 'em. But O. let his grow, and aside from looking a little sacrilegious, they are very becoming to him. . . .

We had, of course, many picturesque experiences, my topnotcher, perhaps, being a late afternoon swim in Lake Sh'ala with the hippopotami coming up to huffle and blow every few minutes, often quite near by. They were not at all alarmed, and we had a very nice swim together! This lake is heavily saline; I was surprised to find hippo in it. They seem, locally, to prefer salt lakes to fresh—there are both kinds adjacent.

It would be hard to pick out the "high spots." In

Long-eared Owl
Asiootus
Holarctic
Pencil drawing
approximately 6" x 4"

the high mountain forests of huge cedars and "olive" trees, a band of blood-winged leaping turacos is no flat affair. The morning water-flight of sand grouse is a stirring sight and a very sporting event of the hot dry lowlands. Five hundred flamingos that don't even move away as the caravan skirts the salt-encrusted beach doesn't need boosting with you as a bird sight, and the same thing, doubled or trebled, seen farther up the lake from a mile-distant camp, swinging up and around and back and forth with the rising sun on their backs and a still-pink sky beyond the mountains across the lake found me short-winded as I forgot to function for the time being. I was afraid I'd be a bit jaded on fillymingos, but there's no danger. I had the same almost unbearable thrill—wide, deep, and full —that my first glimpse gave me, so many years ago, at Grassy Creek. This bird has a different charm—perhaps less wildly beautiful than ours—but it gets you in the same place....

[To his family]

Addis Ababa, Jan. 30, 1927

We all went to tea at Ras Tafari's, quite informally, and were rec'd. quite alone and had a fine time. We took his and the Princess' pictures—still and movie— met, personal, the latest lion cub and cheetah, and I showed him my field studies and asked him to choose a subject for a picture which I wanted to paint for him, to remember our expedition by. He chose a lovely trogon, and I've finished the picture and shall have it framed tomorrow.

[To Mrs. Fuertes and Mary]

Bichana, Gojjam, Feb. 23, 1927

An unexpected chance to get a line to you, as Col. Sanford has a Somali agent here at Ras Hailu's new town, and returns P.D.Q. to Addis.... Ras Hailu, apprised of our approach, had sent a large escort to meet us beyond the Blue Nile, but they went to another crossing ten miles away and we missed them. But he had couriers all along our route, and we established communication before we crossed the river.

It took three more days to reach Bichana, his grandfather's old capital he is now rebuilding. As we approached the last ridge before Bichana, we were met, under a huge fig tree, by the Ras's head Chamberlain and a military escort of five or six hundred, with a Shankalla (slave Negro) band—eight one-piston cornets and six native two-toned flutes, which fell in ahead and conducted us to our camp site, where Hailu had erected a huge tent for our use, with vestibules fore and aft and rugs spread two thick all over the grass inside. He sent word that as it had rained and looked like more, he would postpone his call, but would we all come up tomorrow at 11:30, converse a while and stay to lunch? So, day before yesterday, we all slicked up, and the band was here to blow us up the hill. We passed right through the market and into the palace compound, a double sort of hour-glass shaped affair, with his whole army of 1,000 about equally divided and lined up in two facing rows. As we dismounted and walked up the compound, the rifles were raised and shouldered in advance of us, giving a curious wheely appearance quite impressive.

We had a strictly native lunch of barley-bread, hot

Sooty Shearwater, possibly
Puffinus griseus
Worldwide
Pencil drawing
approximately 4½" x 7"

sauce of gravy and red pepper that would burn out a steel pipe; champagne was the only European touch, which was added to *tej* and barley or wheat beer.

We took all kinds of pictures of him, and on leaving invited him to lunch the next day (yesterday). He came, and our cooks spread themselves and produced a marvelous meal, which he enjoyed hugely. Eight full courses, opened by rum cocktail (rum and pineapple juice and water). After lunch we made a tour of the tents, each man showing his stuff and explaining it. He was much entertained, but really sparkled when the guns were put in his hands. Jack asked if he didn't want to shoot. "Isshe" (Yes), and with three strange rifles made three very good targets—took my shotgun and strolled out to the edge of camp and folded up five kites in five successive shots!! not so bad. After that we had tea in the big tent, and he stayed until nearly an hour after dark, promising a hunt for to-day.

We left camp this a.m. at 7:30 and rode an hour up the country and finally saw a huge crowd a mile up the road. It was Ras Hailu and his retinue, whom we joined, and the whole thousand of us went on, arriving in another half-hour at a very old church he has recently restored. I'll have to *tell* you about that, but it was a top-notcher among all our queer experiences. Here *all* the men and women of the village came out and danced (men together and women and children in another frenzied throng) and sang welcomes to their Ras. Then we went out, only 16 mounted men and about 30 attendants, to hunt reedbuck in the open valley. The Ras killed one—a very good shot, heart, at 75 yards. Approaching another village, more dancers came and danced and shouted before us all

the way in, up to the church, and when we left, escorted us out of the village to a shady acacia grove on the hillside, where the "hunt breakfast" was served—*tej* and barley bread—under a tent, with the entire village dancing and singing outside. We got home about 2 p.m., with the most colorful and bizarre of all our experiences back of us.

Every day since our arrival a procession of food-bearing slaves has come in with bread, bullocks, sheep, chickens, eggs, firewood, and feed for our 60 mules. At the present moment the men are squabbling and quarreling over the apportionment of the day's provender.

This will be our last camp all together.

Khartum, Sudan, April 26, 1927
We are out of Abyssinia, and on our way! The boys met us just before we got to Gallabat, on the *dot!* not an hour lost. . . . No chance of a lion hunt or anything like that, and *all* want to get home as soon as possible.

We've been very successful—3,500 specimens (2,000 birds)—had *no* sickness nor serious trouble with the men; the Simien boys got thirteen ibex, including four fine bucks—one an inch short of the record.

I am awfully glad you're with Sheila and D. K. [Mr. and Mrs. David Kennedy-Fraser, in Milngavie, Scotland] and it is quite likely that O. and I will come up to Glasgow and sail from there. We shall be here a week, then right down to Cairo and out, overland to England, put in a few days at the Brit. Museum, and then "Ho for Glesgie."

THE PLATES

Although some oil paintings have been included, the majority of the pictures reproduced in this book are water colors, wash drawings, and pencil sketches. These, for the most part, are Fuertes' first impressions of birds, made in his field sketches or done shortly after he returned to his studio. Not all of Fuertes' water colors and drawings were done in this way, however. The great majority, in fact, perhaps as many as two thousand, are like his oils, formal portraits of birds prepared as illustrations for books, magazines, and ornithological journals. These are the "plates" to which I refer in the Biographical Essay. The formal (and to me less interesting) quality of these plates was one reason for not including many of them in this book. Another was the fact that most of those originals have long been exposed to the light, hanging in homes or offices or circulating through the country on exhibition. As a result, their colors have faded and, in some instances, have almost disappeared. The drawings and water colors reproduced here have not suffered from such overexposure to light or from careless handling. Most have been locked up in safes and vaults for many years, and their original colors survive unimpaired. Through this book, which confines itself to these paintings, withheld from general view so many years, it is hoped that the public will finally have an opportunity to view and to judge Louis Agassiz Fuertes' abilities as an artist.

It will be quickly apparent on looking through the plates that they vary immensely in style. On some of his work Fuertes lavished great care—for example, the Great Horned Owl (plate 9) and the Potoo (plate 10). Others he dashed off in a few minutes, rapidly recording his impressions of parts of a bird that might lose their color after death, as in the sketch of the Stone Curlew (plate 23).

Plates 1 and 2 are from the period of Fuertes' earliest work, about 1895 to 1897, when he was developing his own adaptation of Audubon's style, and they are good examples of his beginning attempts. During this time Fuertes often used pen and ink to heighten the effect of water color. Mary Fuertes Boynton tells me that her father gave up this technique because it put too great a strain on his eyes. The influence of Abbott Thayer, with whom Fuertes began to study in 1897, may also have persuaded him to change his style. The results of his study and the changes in his style after the passage of two years can be seen in the picture of the Red-tailed Hawk (plate 3).

Plates 4 to 14 represent Fuertes working in a variety of styles over a period of some years before 1922 and, for the most part, before 1915. The majority of these paintings are fairly formal portraits, and in some cases, such as those of the Golden Woodpecker (plate 8) and the Hybrid Quail (plate 13), the backgrounds are highly developed. In at least one instance, that of the White Gyrfalcon (plate 6) the portrait is almost monumental, the pose and background color idealized to an extent not seen in most of the paintings reproduced here.

Plates 15 to 19 were painted in Fuertes' studio about 1903, in connection with a projected work on the birds of Mexico. Mrs. Boynton says that her father did not think well of these pictures, but I chose to include them, however disrespectful this may seem, because I think they are interesting examples of another style. These paintings tend to contrast with Fuertes' other work because of the attention he gave here to the whole composition. Each bird is placed in its natural setting and much care has been taken to establish a relationship between the form of the bird and the patterns Fuertes created in the surrounding foliage. Plates 17 and 19 show this well. In the one the rounded body of the Crimson-collared Tanager is repeated in the trunk of the palm tree on which it rests; in the other the crest of the Magpie Jay has a counterpart in the forms of some of the plants.

Fuertes' paintings from his Abyssinian journey (plates 20 to 33) were executed in late 1926 and early 1927, the last year of his life. He was very pleased with them. My colleague Pro-

fessor Henry Guerlac, then a young man who had worked with Fuertes, met him shortly after his return from Abyssinia. Fuertes was carrying his bundle of Abyssinian sketches. Calling Guerlac over, Fuertes sat down at the edge of the sidewalk, feet in the gutter, and the two, as Fuertes would have said, gloated over the pictures as traffic and pedestrians passed by. Fuertes painted about a hundred pictures during this journey, and all of them have tremendous boldness and immediacy. The bird is always there, alive. The selections here show his sense of color, form, and texture and the skill with which he conveyed the life and individuality of the bird or mammal he was painting. He turned from the rounded softness of Bruce's Green Pigeon (plate 25) to the power of the Fish Eagle (plate 29), from the compact, downy structure of the Curly-crested Helmet Shrike (plate 26), to the loose streaming feathers on the crest and neck of the Secretary Bird (plate 27).

Plates 34 to 52 are an interesting group. Fuertes painted them at different times in his career, the earliest in 1899, and almost all of them were in his possession at the time of his death. A comparison of these water colors with the others reproduced here shows an element of informality and experimentation. In some instances, for example plates 40 and 49, Fuertes is in a playful mood; in plate 46, on the other hand, a particular feature, the beauty of a color, has caught his eye; in plate 42 he saw the opportunity for a spectacular composition. These paintings appear to represent Fuertes when he was most relaxed and trying his hand at different styles. He may very well have kept these pictures because he had a special fondness for them.

From time to time Fuertes painted in oils, usually on commission. These works, here represented by plates 53 through 60, are generally more studied and formally composed. The outstanding examples, which Fuertes considered his best work in oil, are 24 portraits of game birds, shore birds, waterfowl, and birds of prey, which he painted for Frederick F. Brewster in 1910–1911. Brewster had in his New Haven, Connecticut, home a large teak-paneled room—the Edgerton Study, he called it. Fuertes designed his paintings for the panels on the study walls. They painted easily. In a letter to Chapman in January, 1911, Fuertes remarked how they just "slid onto the canvas." Brewster's will provided that after his death and the death of his wife, their home should be demolished and the paneling of the Edgerton Study moved to Ithaca, New York, where it would be reassembled as a setting for the Fuertes paintings. Cornell University added the Brewster wing to the Lyman K. Stuart Observatory, headquarters of the University's Laboratory of Ornithology, and in the reassembled Fuertes Room the original pictures are on permanent display. Plates 53 to 58 are from the Fuertes Room; 59 is from the corridor exhibition area in the observatory. Fuertes painted plate 60, to which Roger Tory Peterson refers in his introduction, as a gift to his fraternity, Alpha Delta Phi.

In selecting the artwork for this book, I have depended almost entirely on my own judgment, using as the sole standard the quality of the paintings and drawings as works of art. I have not tried to make the selection representative of different species of birds, and have, in fact, included three mammal portraits (plates 32, 33, and 45) to show something of Fuertes' extraordinary versatility.

I think that these plates represent Fuertes at his full power as an artist. Here are the field sketches, the formal portraits, the life studies. Above all, here is the work of a lover of birds, who had the ability to translate his knowledge into brilliant re-creations, down to the subtlest texture of a bird's feathers or to the gleam of its eye. These are not the works of a romantic or a sentimentalist; the paintings are frank and free, and some of the birds almost leap off the page into life. Fuertes had the feel of birds in his eye and in his hand, and his work is not only a triumph of bird art but a rich evocation of and tribute to birds themselves.

Plate 1
Green Woodpecker
Picus viridus
Europe
Watercolor with pen and ink; 15" x 11"
about 1896

Green Woodpecker.
- Picus viridis -

Plate 2

Common Snipe
Capello gallinago
North America
Watercolor with pen and ink; 11″ x 15″
about 1896

American or "English" Snipe.
♂ (Gallinago Wilsonii) ♀

Plate 3
Red-tailed Hawk
Buteo jamaicensis
North America
Watercolor; 15" x 11"
1899

Red Tailed Hawk
Buteo borealis ♂ ad
"Ithaca, Sep. 10, '99.

Plate 4

Snowy Owl
Nyctea scandiaca
Holarctic
Watercolor; 15" x 11"
no date, but before 1915

Louis Agassiz Fuertes.

Plate 5

Bullock's Oriole
Icterus bullockii abeiller
Western North America
Watercolor; 15″ x 11″
no date, but before 1915

Louis Agassiz Fuertes.

Plate 6
White Gyrfalcon
Falco rusticolus
Holarctic
Watercolor; 15" x 11"
1922

Plate 7
Sage Grouse
Centrocercus urophasianus
Western North America
Watercolor; 11" x 15"
1926

-Sage-Cock-
Wattman, Wyo.
Jan 6, 1926-
-Robt. Grieve-

Plate 8
Golden Woodpecker
Dinopium javanese
Southeast Asia
Watercolor; 15" x 11"
no date

Plate 9
Great Horned Owl
Bubo virginianus
North America
Watercolor; 22" x 15"
no date, but before 1915

Plate 10

Common Potoo
Nictibius griseus
Central and South America
Watercolor; 22" x 15"
no date, but before 1915

Plate 11
Eastern Kingbird
Tyrannus tyrannus
Eastern North America
Watercolor; 15" x 11"
no date, but before 1915

Louis Agassiz Fuertes.

Plate 12
Sharp-shinned Hawk
Accipiter striatus
North America
Watercolor; 11" x 15"
no date

Louis A. Fuertes.

Plate 13
Hybrid Quail (Gambel X Scaled)
Lophortyx gambelli X Callipepla squamata
Western North America
Watercolor; 22″ x 15″
1916

Louis Agassiz Fuertes,

Hybrid— | Callipepla s. squamata. ♂
           | Lophortyx gambeli.
Grant Co., New Mexico, Nov. 26, 1916

Plate 14
Shama Thrush
Copsicus malabaricus
India and Burma
Watercolor; 11" x 15"
no date, but before 1915

Louis Agassiz Fuertes.

Plate 15
Agami Heron
Agamia agami
Central and South America
Watercolor; 15" x 11"
1903

Plate 22
African Swallow-tailed Kite
Chelictinia riocourii
Africa
Watercolor; 15" x 11"
1927

Mt. Guramba - Sidamo -
Dre 24, 1926 -

Haploderma n. narina -

Swallow-Kite.
(Chelictinia riocourii)

Near Matemma.
APRIL 15, 1927.
(A·M·B·)

Plate 23

Stone Curlew
Burhinus oedicnemus
Europe and Africa
Watercolor; 11" x 15"
1927

Oedicnemis (or Burhinus) senegalensis.
Gidu River- Sake Shiala.
Jan 5 - 1927.
(Legs pale yellow-green - dull)

Plate 24

Black-headed Heron
Ardea melanocephala
Africa
Watercolor; 15" x 11"
1927

Bichana, Gojam-
Feb. 20, 1927-

Ardea melanocephala.

Plate 25
Bruce's Green Pigeon
Treron waalia
Africa
Watercolor; 11" x 15"
1927

Vinago waalia.

Green Fig Pigeon.

Lake Leva

Jan. 13 - 1927

Plate 26
Curly-crested Helmet Shrike
Prionops cristata
Africa
Watercolor; 15" x 11"
1927

15 MILES WEST
OF
LAKE T'SANA.
- APRIL 6, 1927 -

Prionops concinnata

Plate 27
Secretary Bird
Sagittarius serpentarius
Africa
Watercolor; 11" x 15"
1927

Secretary-Bird.

Sagittarius
Serpentarius.

Dangela.
Gojam-
Mar. 25, 1927.

Plate 28
Cape Teal
Anas capensis
South Africa
Watercolor; 11" x 15"
1927

Hora Alpuata -
Jan 8, 1927 -

Nettion capense -

Plate 29
Fish Eagle (juvenile)
Cuncuma vocifer
Africa
Watercolor; 15" x 11"
1927

Bulbula River
Lake Zwai

Jan 12 - 1927-

Cuncuma vocifer
Imm

Plate 30
Hoopoe
Upupa epops
Europe and Africa
Watercolor; 15" x 11"
1927

20 Miles North-west
of Lake T'sana,
~April 6. 1927~

Hoopoe

Upupa epops ~

Plate 31

Spur-winged Goose
Plectropterus gambensis
Africa
Watercolor; 15" x 11"
1927

Plectropterus gambensis.

-Lake T'sana-
April 4.
-1927-

Plate 32
Abyssinian Wolf
Canis simensis
Africa
Watercolor; 11" x 15"
1926

"Kabaru"
(Canis simensis)
MT. Albasso.
Nov. 11, 1926
W. H. O.

Plate 33
Gelada Baboon
Theropithecus gelada
Africa
Watercolor; 11" x 15"
1926

GELADA BABOON.
MUGGER CAÑON RIM. at "MULU".
A.W.B.   Oct 21, 1925.

Plate 34
Magnificent Frigate Bird
Fregata magnificens
North Central Pacific, Central Atlantic, Caribbean
Watercolor; 11" x 15"
about 1900

Man-o-War

Plate 35

Willow Ptarmigan
Lagopus lagopus
North America
Watercolor; 11" x 15"
1899

Fuertes

Willow Ptarmigan
June 20 99
Yakutat Bay

Willow Ptarmigan

Plate 36
Pileated Woodpecker
Dryocopus pileatus
North America
Watercolor; 15" x 11"
1903

Pileated Woodpecker
Jan 6 - 1903.   North Carolina

Plate 37

Bald Eagle (juvenile)
Haliaeetus leucocephalus
North America
Watercolor; 11" x 15"
about 1900

Plate 38
Wilson's Phalarope
Steganopus tricolor
North America
Watercolor; 11" x 15"
1903

Wilson's Phalarope　　　Los Baños, June 21

Plate 39
Chestnut-eared Aracari
Pteroglossus castanotis canastotis
South America
Watercolor; 11" x 15"
1913

Villavicencia.
Mar 12, 1913

Pteroglossus castanotis.

Plate 40
Common Peacock
Pavo cristatus
India and Burma
Watercolor; 11" x 15"
no date

Plate 41
Roseate Spoonbill
Ajaia ajaia
Florida, Texas, Central America,
Northern South America
Watercolor; 15" x 11"
1910

Pajaro Island
Tamialusa Lagoon Tampico, Mex.

Roseate Spoonbill

L.A.F.

Plate 42
Lesser Bird of Paradise
Paradisaea minor
New Guinea
Watercolor; 15" x 11"
1920

P. minor - Bronx, Mar 1, 1920

Plate 43
Hoatzin
Opisthocomus hoazin
Northern South America
Watercolor; 15" x 11"
1913

Hoatzin -

Opisthocomus

Villavicencio,
Colombia

Hoatzin.

Opisthocomus hoazin.

Villavicencio. Col., May 11, 1913

(T.M.R.)

Plate 44
Horned Grebe (juvenile)
Podiceps auritus
Holarctic
Watercolor; 15" x 11"
1909

Big Hill Pond
Dast Cape Mag. Isd.
Aug. 31, 1909.

Young Horned Grebe —

Plate 45
Antelope Jack Rabbit
Lepus alleni
North America
Watercolor; 11" x 15"
1901

Texas Jack Rabbit

Marathon, Tex. 1901

Plate 46
Louisiana Heron
Hydranassa tricolor
North America
Watercolor; 7½" x 11"
no date

Plate 47
Poorwill
Phalaenoptilus nuttallii
Western North America
Watercolor; 11" x 15"
1901

Poor-Will

Comstock. Apr. 21, 1941

Plate 48
Wild Turkey
Meleagris gallopavo
North America
Watercolor; 7½" x 11"
no date

Plate 49
Black-necked Stilt (juvenile)
Himantopus mexicanus
North America
Watercolor; 15" x 11"
1903

Los Baños
June 19 - 03

Stilt

Plate 50
Citreoline Trogon
Trogon citreolus melanocephalus
Central America
Watercolor; 15" x 11"
1910

Trogon

Trogon melanocephalus
(#2233)
Tampico, Mex.

Plate 51
Long-billed Curlew
Numenius americanus
North America
Watercolor; 11" x 15"
1901

Langtry, Apr. 24.

Plate 52
Great Blue Heron
Ardea herodias
North America
Watercolor; 11" x 15"
1908

Great Blue Heron.   Ithaca, N.y. Oct 30, 1908.
                                        (Geo. Foote)

Plate 53
Red-shouldered Hawk
Buteo lineatus
North America
Oil; 36" x 29"
1910

Plate 54
Ruffed Grouse
Bonasa umbellus
Eastern North America
Oil; 36" x 29"
1910

Plate 55
Oldsquaws
Clangula hyemalis
Holarctic
Oil; 36" x 20½"
1910

Louis Agassiz Fuertes.
1910

Plate 56

Wild Turkey
Meleagris gallopavo
North America
Oil; 36" x 26½"
1910

Louis Agassiz Fuertes
1910

Plate 57

Peregrine Falcon
Falco peregrinus anatum
Holarctic
Oil; 36" x 23"
1910

Plate 58
Gyrfalcon
Falco rusticolus
Holarctic
Oil; 36" x 24½"
1910

Plate 59

Canvasbacks
Aythya valisineria
Holarctic
Oil; 21½" x 34"
no date

Plate 60
Great Horned Owl
Bubo virginianus
North America
Oil; 25" x 39"
1925, or slightly earlier

A Fuertes bibliography

The basic source of information on Fuertes and his work is Mary Fuertes Boynton's *Louis Agassiz Fuertes, His Life Briefly Told and His Correspondence Edited* (New York: Oxford University Press, 1956). This book by Fuertes' daughter contains, among other things, extensive quotations from his letters, a list of books and articles that he illustrated, a list of the principal collections of his paintings and drawings (except those belonging to Mrs. Boynton and her brother), and a bibliography of books and articles about Fuertes and by him. Most of the works listed below are also in that bibliography.

Album of Abyssinian Birds and Mammals from Paintings by Louis Agassiz Fuertes, introduction by Wilfred Hudson Osgood. Chicago, Ill.: Field Museum of Natural History, 1930.

Allen, Arthur Augustus. "The Passing of a Great Teacher," *Bird-Lore,* Vol. XXIX (1927), pp. 372–376.

Boynton, Mary Fuertes. "Louis Agassiz Fuertes," *The New York State Conservationist,* Vol. VII, No. 4 (1954), pp. 10–12. New York State Conservation Department.

Chapman, Frank. *Camps and Cruises of an Ornithologist.* New York: D. Appleton and Company, 1908.

———. *Autobiography of a Bird Lover.* New York: D. Appleton and Company, 1933.

———. "A Great Portrait Painter of Birds," *Bird-Lore,* Vol. XVII (1915), pp. 277–284.

———. "Louis Agassiz Fuertes, 1874–1927," *Bird-Lore,* Vol. XXIX (1927), pp. 359–368.

———. "In Memoriam: Louis Agassiz Fuertes, 1874–1927," *The Auk,* Vol. XLV (1928), pp. 1–26.

———. "Fuertes and Audubon," *Natural History,* Vol. XLII (1937), pp. 205–213.

———. "Memories of Louis Fuertes," *Bird-Lore,* Vol. XLI (1939), pp. 3–10.

Drahos, Nick. "Early Fuertes Paintings Come Home," *The Conservationist,* Vol. XXII (1968), pp. 26–27. State of New York Department of Environmental Conservation.

Eckelberry, Don Richard. "Birds in Art and Illustration," in Olin Sewell Pettingill, Jr., ed., *The Living Bird, Second Annual, 1963.* Ithaca, N.Y.: Laboratory of Ornithology, Cornell University, 1963, pp. 69–82.

Fuertes, Louis Agassiz. "Impressions of the Voices of Tropical Birds," *Bird-Lore,* Vol. XV (1913), pp. 341–344; Vol. XVI (1914), pp. 1–4, 96–101, 161–169, 342–349, 421–428.

——— and Osgood, Wilfred Hudson. *Artist and Naturalist in Ethiopia.* Garden City, N.Y.: Doubleday, Doran Company, 1936.

Hadley, Alden H. "With Fuertes in Florida," *American Forests,* Vol. XXXVII (1931), pp. 71–73 and 128.

Howes, Paul Griswold. *Photographer in the Rain-Forests.* Chicago, Ill.: Paul G. Howes and Associates, Adams Press, 1969.

Marcham, Frederick George. "Louis Fuertes Revisited," in Olin Sewell Pettingill, Jr., ed., *The Living Bird, Second Annual, 1963*. Ithaca, N.Y.: Laboratory of Ornithology, Cornell University, 1963, pp. 83–92.

Osgood, Wilfred Hudson. "Louis Agassiz Fuertes," *Science,* Vol. LXVI (1927), pp. 469–472.

Palmer, Ephraim Lawrence. "Louis Agassiz Fuertes," *Nature Magazine,* Vol. XII (1928), pp. 177–179.

Sutton, George Miksch. "Louis Fuertes, Teacher," *Audubon Magazine,* Vol. XLII (1941), pp. 521–524.

———. "Louis Fuertes at Work," *Audubon Magazine,* Vol. XLIV (1942), pp. 37–40.

———. "Fuertes and the Young Bird Artist," *ibid.,* pp. 82–85.

Wells, David I. "Drawing Wild Birds in Their Native Haunts. A Sketch of the Personality and Methods of Louis Agassiz Fuertes, the Bird Artist," *The Outing Magazine,* Vol. LIV (1909), pp. 565–573.

Index

Numbers in italics refer to illustrations or plates: *25, plate 44*.

Collections

COLOR PLATES